Recognition

It is with the greatest gratitude that I dedicate this book to:

The glory of the Lord Jesus Christ

Who taught me and continues daily to teach me how impact the world and the people and the businesses around me through the uncommon way He develops and leads me. At times His knowledge is greater than my ability to comprehend and to present to you.

Janice

My wife whom I love and adore with the love God Himself has given to me.

Derek and Dawn, Marcus, Jered and Seth

Our precious sons and daughter-in-law, whose lives have inspired me to live in the grace God has given me for their example and blessing.

God's Greater Community of Interest

My church family, the community of people, businesses and other organizations around me that are at the heart of God's desire for them to live and to prosper in His favor.

Footprints   A Leader's Message

It First Starts In You!

    The truly great leaders all have this one thing in common – each will have a compelling message to be delivered to all those who come within their reach. The leader's message is probably spoken only on rare occasions but it is lived daily. You have met these people I'm sure. When you meet them they open your eyes to realities you never knew about things you never knew. They leave you with a burning inside that says to you *it starts in me!*

    Footprints is the expression of my message to you; that uncommon people have uncommon ways and create uncommon impact because they have learned everything starts in them before it is started with them. Becoming a leader of uncommon significance must be in you before it can come from you.

    The story of another uncommon leader goes this way. Sometime, close to a battlefield over 200 years ago, a man in civilian clothes rode past a small group of exhausted battle-weary soldiers digging an obviously important defensive position. The section leader, making no effort to help, was shouting orders and threatening punishment if the work was not completed within the hour. *Why are you are not helping?* asked the stranger on horseback.

    I am in charge. The men do as I tell them, said the section leader, adding, *Help them yourself if you feel strongly about it.* To the section leader's surprise the stranger dismounted and helped the

Footprints   A Leader's Message

men until the job was finished.   Before leaving the stranger congratulated the men for their work, and approached the puzzled section leader. *You should notify top command next time your rank prevents you from supporting your men - and I will provide a more permanent solution,* said the stranger.

Up close, the section leader now recognized the man was General Washington. He caught the lesson he'd just been taught. His message – nothing your people are asked to do should be beyond you to do yourself - great leadership starts in you more than with you. That is my message to you; that is my encouragement to you; that is my challenge to you. *It Starts Within You!*

Table of Contents

Recognition I
It First Starts In You! II
Table of Contents IV
Common Leadership 1
Stages of Uncommon Development 23
Developing Healthy Leadership Perspectives 26
Preparing for Leadership 51
Uncommon Development Below The Surface 69
From Influence to Association 91
Developing an Effective Leadership Style 109
An Uncommon Leader's Job Announcement 130
Developed to Last 178
The Stages of Uncommon Development 224
Footprints of Maturation 227
Footprints of Qualification 234
Footprints of Collaboration 239
Footprints of Determination 252
The Footprints of Transformation 266
Conclusion 276
The Power of – PDP® 281

Common Leadership

"When your leadership is approved by others the results will be more leaders than followers along your path".
Footprints

Before my son's basketball season began the coaches talked with the parents and shared that their primary objective for the boys was to continue developing them to become young leaders. They explained to us that the games would be the tool they used to create an environment where the boys could start learning to lead, to influence and to encourage one another in positive ways. As the parents, our roles were to support and to encourage the boys; they were a group of 14-15 year olds who were just learning what it really meant to be self-disciplined. Learning to lead by becoming a contributing part of a cohesive team was a big step of development for them.

To put the boys and the parents in the right frame of mind for the season, the coaches asked me to tell them a story of leadership and teamwork and what it really meant to lead well. I decided to tell them the story of why flocks of geese fly in a V formation.

As a flock of geese takes flight from a shoreline, heading north for the summer or south for the winter, they lift off from the water in a squawking discourse. Yet, in a matter of seconds, a line begins to emerge from the mass of brown feathers. This line straightens, arches slightly and then, as on cue, bends sharply to form a perfect V shape. Geese fly in V formation for a very pragmatic reason: a flock of geese flying in formation can move faster and maintain flight longer than any one goose flying alone. They learn to use the synergy of the group to their advantage.

The formation helps them conserve their energy. Each bird flies slightly above the bird in front of him, resulting in a reduction of wind resistance. Each bird takes turns leading by being in the front, falling back when they get tired. In this way, the geese can fly for a long time before they must stop for rest. In fact it's believed that as a group, geese can fly up to 70% longer than when they are alone.

Flying in the V formation also makes it easy to keep track of every bird in the group. It helps with communication and coordination within the group. While the lead goose is out front those behind him honk with encouragement. Each bird is developed to take the lead position at some point so they are a flock of leaders. The bird in the lead position must select a pace that is best for the entire group; it must also be able to choose the best course and direction for the group.

The bird in the lead position expends more energy than the others so each bird is developed to support others when not in the lead. When a bird gets tired or sick and must drop back or out of the formation at least two birds stay with him. If a sick bird must land to rest, his support will land and stay with him until the sick bird is able to fly again. Finally, geese fly in a V formation because it allows them to see what one another is doing and to encourage each other to keep working together and to discourage or correct one another when one may do something harmful to itself or to the flock. The geese are a great example of leadership and teamwork at work.

The boys really received the story well; it was a great idea of the coaches to do this. When the season started most of our kids were still learning to deal effectively with the self; now we wanted them to develop interpersonal effectiveness with other young people too! It was a lot to ask and to expect of them but then good things don't always come to us easily.

Learning to lead effectively takes time; we wanted to start the development process with the boys while they were young and in their formative years when they typically discover and decide on the persons they want to grow up to be. Life isn't set up to give young people an easy road to positive development, so we wanted to create an environment that would give them as many positive experiences as the negative experiences they are sure to see and experience in the world. Our examples as parent leaders would be important to the effective development of the boys.

While attending one of the games the father of one of my son's teammates sat on the bleacher seat next to me. I had seen him before at other games but I had never really met him. Today I learned his name was Watson. He was a big man, probably 6'4" and perhaps weighing well over 250 pounds; when he walked by no one in the gym could miss him because of his size. But today Watson made himself known to most everyone in the gym not because of his size but because his behavior.

Watson sat right next to me on a seat perched four rows back from the basketball floor. And from there he acted like a still maturing 14 year old in the body of a 45 year old adult. You see, Watson yelled incessantly to the boys, the coaches and even the game officials, *shoot the ball; call time out; that was a foul; how could you miss that call?; why did you call that play?*

It was clear to most everyone there that Watson wasn't just trying to encourage and support the boys; he was trying to direct the boys. His behavior was extremely disruptive to the boys, to the coaches and to the game officials.

About half way through the game, I gazed at Watson the same way I gaze at my kids when I want them to know they should change their behaviors. My kids call it *The Look*. I bet every parent has a look that in some instances communicates more powerfully and more clearly than words. When Watson saw this look on my face he said to me *I'm just a bottom line guy; I just want to do all that I can do to help these boys win; you have to get out front to lead.*

He reasoned however that we all thought he should quiet down a bit. I was thinking something entirely different! Watson misread how I perceived his actions like he probably was accustomed to misreading how others perceived him. I asked him to tell me, *if you were the coaches; if you were the officials; if you were the players and if you were the other parents and spectators how would you react to yourself? If you were on the receiving end of your own behavior how would you respond?*

After a moment of deep thought, a look of embarrassment came over him. I could tell that he was torn. He realized his behavior said a lot more about him than what he intended. He learned that people identified with and remembered the unintended things about him that he would rather they didn't know. Was he encouraging or aggressive? Was he supporting or controlling? Did he want our boys to win and the other boys to lose?

Watson was thinking *how could he follow himself*? He thought that if he couldn't follow himself then who else would. Watson is like many people who battle with themselves and against others to pursue a bottom line approach to life, work and pleasure. People like this will devote their lives to perfecting a dominating controlling approach to getting what they desire. It's an approach that works well when all is directed at the self but when others are involved it is terribly ineffective. Positive people do not generally react constructively to a controlling and directing type behavior especially from a leader.

This type of leading is similar to the dominate stallion in a heard of wild horses; the stallion leads and the other horses follow. Achieving success is an easier task for the stallion than maintaining success. Each day the stallion must fight to preserve its lead position among other stallions who want to be the leader. Each day the lead stallion must keep his heard under tighter control than the day before. Imagine how exhausting this must be for the lead stallion and for the heard; rival stallions patiently wait for the day and time when the lead stallion is most vulnerable from the exhausting work of maintaining its lead position out front. Then they make their challenge to overthrow his leadership.

Dominate bottom line leading may work with horses but it will never be effective with people or in businesses or in any social, public or professional setting where more than one person is involved. It is always more difficult over time to achieve and maintain success with bottom line leading. The approach places far too much emphasis on the strength of the leader than on the development and value of those who are led.

Similarly, Watson's leading and encouragement as he put it, actually worked against the objectives of the coaches, the officials and the team. The bottom line objective with the team was development. The game was simply the tool coaching leaders used to develop the leadership of the boys; winning the game was to them a byproduct of winning the battle to put these young kids on a path that would enable each of them to develop more effective personal leadership. Watson's behavior was more appropriate for developing people to be good at following instructions. We wanted the boys to learn to be great examples of young leaders; we were not looking for examples of great followers.

Footprints   Leading Beyond Your Limits

Our leadership should be for the benefit of others – never for our own aspirations.

Watson and I got to know each other beyond the games because I went on to work with him and his business associates helping him to develop his effectiveness as a leader. I learned in the weeks and months after the basketball season that Watson had developed his style of leading because he thought every effective leader focused on first being first; to him becoming better was achieved because you learned to be first.

It's too bad someone didn't get to Watson while he was a 14 year old, to help develop his idea of leading and ultimately the style of leading he would choose for himself as an adult. His was an immature way to pursue and to develop effective personal leadership. And it's the type of leading that is most often rejected by others. Watson learned that when your leadership is approved by others the results will be more leaders than followers along your path.

Leading happens when we dictate and control what we want others to do; but leadership happens when we develop and transform who we want others to be. This is one of the reasons I decided to write this book. Most of us want to be leaders at some time in our lives; it's a personal sense of progression and development. But our leadership is more important to others and to the businesses and institutions we support than the act of leading is to us personally. People who want to be effective leaders are probably aware of the book "Seven Habits of Highly Effective People". Most of us understand that a leader must have emotional intelligence; most of us understand that some competencies are more critical than others for leadership success.

We can recognize effective habits; we can recognize when we have or do not have emotional intelligence; and we can identify the competencies critical to leading others. But what we miss is learning how these things work together for our effectiveness. Let me ask you a question. How do we recognize effective leadership from ineffective leadership? (See page 23 for the answer to this question).

Watson's initial approach to leadership was fairly common with people. You probably know them. They try to take charge to be in charge; they get out front to lead; they want to be the first as much as possible; and they push and drive others. It's an ineffective way to lead. It was inappropriate for kids who were just learning about themselves; and it's inappropriate for mature people who routinely need to unlearn bad habits they have already developed about leading. I don't think the common way of leading would even work with a flock of geese.

I believe we are at time and place where we cannot afford to wait to be led or misled by the ineffectiveness of a common approach to leadership. I wrote Footprints for people who want to develop more leaders around them. It is written for businesses and teams and organizations that want to develop people to be more leaders than followers and for people who want to achieve more long term lasting successes. It is written for individuals who don't want to go through life always being led by others but who want to become more effective leading themselves, influencing their leaders and influencing results from wherever and whatever their circumstance may be at the time. It is written for those who want to go from common to uncommon leadership.

Becoming an uncommon leader is possible for anyone who is willing learn why they must change, what they must change and how to change things about themselves that hinder effectiveness with others. Watson did it! The way to becoming an uncommon leader is more a path taken than an act accomplished. Footprints describe an uncommon journey taking an uncommon path to developing uncommon effectiveness in leading yourself and in leading others. It's your time to lift off, elevate, form a V formation with those around you and start your journey to becoming an uncommon leader of uncommon people!

Where and When Development Starts

"If your actions inspire others to dream more, learn more, do more and become more, you are probably a leader".
John Quincy Adams

The Uncommon Leader

I conduct leadership development and strategic planning seminars for businesses and individuals all over the United States and internationally. I often ask the question *where did you learn to be the leader you are today?* I don't really expect an answer. The purpose of the question is to invite reflection on what really makes a person a leader and what makes a leader uncommon. In a group of 25 people, I might get 25 different responses. Remember Watson had an immature perspective of what a leader really was. He was a bottom line guy. To him being the first to be first is what made him a leader. In his professional life profit was his first priority; in his private life winning was his first priority; and in his social life he believed being first professionally and privately would carry over to his being first with and among others.

All this changed for Watson when he realized he really wouldn't have enjoyed working for himself; he realized he was missing something

If being first is important to you then it should be paramount to be the first to put the needs of others first.

about being a leader that was greater than just being first. When being first is the measure of your effectiveness then your customers, vendors and competitors will measure you by what you do to become first; and your family, friends, coworkers and associates will measure you by what you do when you are first. Being first may make you the leader among those like you; but being first for others will make you uncommon with those that matter most!

Some of our most respected leaders, Nelson Mandela, Martin Luther King Jr., Abraham Lincoln, were really just common people with uncommon ways among common men. So what is it that made them uncommon? Well it's probably not what we think and it's more than we think. Let me explain. When we see leaves blowing across the yard; when we feel the cold wind blow across our face we say *look at the wind; it is strong today.* But we cannot really see the wind; we see only the results of what the wind does. It's difficult if not impossible to adequately describe wind without describing what winds does and how it acts.

We have a similar challenge when we want to describe leadership. We've got lots of books, teachings and training that describe leadership by placing an almost singular importance on results the leader achieves and or on the results we believe the leader should achieve. Results are definitely and inherently part of what make a leader effective. But so are qualities such as influence, intelligence, determination, vision. All are required for the success of the leader but they are insufficient to describe what makes a leader.

Daniel Goleman is known for identifying factors of emotional intelligence that are critical to what makes a leader successful. Goleman's five components of emotional intelligence are: Self-Awareness; Self-Regulation; Motivation; Empathy; and Social Skill. He notes that his research shows these five components of emotional intelligence are the sine qua non of leadership – the bottom line so to speak. Without it, a person can have the best training in the world, an incisive analytical mind and an endless supply of smart ideas, but he still would not make a leader. Watson probably failed the test of self-awareness, self-regulation, motivation, empathy and social skill. Goleman's components of emotional intelligence are a good place to start in determining what makes a leader; they suggest something more than just results.

Footprints - It First Starts Within!

Think about this. What makes a leader may be the things we do within ourselves to win the battle to first be an effective leader of ourselves. Using Goleman's five components of emotional intelligence let me explain what I mean by first leading the self. Do I make myself aware of how I impact others – self-aware; do I hold myself responsible for disruptive emotions I may have – self-regulation; do I have a passion for what I do that goes beyond money or status - motivation; do I have the heart to understand the emotional makeup of others - empathy; and do I have the ability to build positive relationships with others – social skill? This view suggests that what makes a leader is what goes on within a person that forms the reason or basis for the things we see a person accomplish.

We now know that only $1/10^{th}$ of the iceberg that caused the Titanic to sink was visible to us. A full $9/10^{th}$ of the iceberg was below the surface of the water! It's estimated the part of the iceberg we saw was probably 50 to 100 feet high and 200 to 400 feet long. So you can see (no pun here), what we saw we called an iceberg but what we didn't see beneath the surface of the ocean made it an uncommon iceberg.

Results a leader achieves are above the surface of things; they only tell us a leader is around. But what really makes a leader is perhaps what we do not see; that which is sewn in the depths of our lives deep below the surface of what we see.

Chapter One

Consider this. If in all the world there was only one person, the world and that person would still require a leader. If you were that person, would you be that leader? What we are able to do with ourselves is where leadership starts and it is perhaps the best indication of what we should be able to do with others. How you lead yourself is of greater importance and has a greater impact on your success and the success of those around you than anything else in life.

So then, if you were the only person alive what results would you achieve that would adequately identify you as a leader? And how would you describe those results in such a way that they have meaning and value to the world? Uncommon leadership starts first with you and it culminates in the lives of those around you and in the businesses in which you operate.

I once played a round of golf with a Marine Corps General. I am not a golfer but I play golf respectably – not great but not terribly either. My boss, who was an Army General himself, invited me to play with him and a Marine Corps General. I had the privilege, so I thought before the round began, of riding in the cart with the Marine General. I quickly learned that he played golf much like he probably did anything. The golf ball was his enemy, the golf clubs were his weapons and the golf course was the battlefield. For 18 intense holes of golf this general beat one golf ball after another to the point of surrender.

To take his mind off the game at one point during the day, I asked him how many weeks it took to make a person a Marine. He stopped the golf cart for a moment, looked at me and said *we don't make Marines. People join the Marine Corps; but they must choose to become Marines and this can take as little time as a day or as long as a career for them to have the sense to realize it and the will to do it.*

I was at a loss for what to say because of the profound nature of his statement. You see even then, long before I decided to write this book, that General was describing a leader by what happened below the surface of life; by the inputs a person must make rather than the outcomes the person achieves. And when you think about it, each day people from every aspect of life are challenged to make the decision to be something that achieving something or doing something can never make them. Wearing the uniform and being trained; holding the position; or having the status is insufficient to make me, you or anyone else a leader.

The path to developing uncommon effectiveness starts first with will rather than with skill.

Like a Marine, becoming a leader is a choice each of us must make; first for our own lives and the circumstances we want to drive and then about how we give our lives to enabling the success of others around us.

Wanting to be identified as a leader but not preparing for the role is like having a wedding but failing to cultivate the marriage. The wedding happens at the church with lots of people to see but

Leadership first starts within us, then with us!

the marriage happens in your life where only you and your spouse really know if you are committed to it. I believe it's the same with leadership; what ultimately makes us leaders is that which is sown within us which gives rise to and sustains what is seen outside of us. What makes you the leader you are today? How did you develop yourself to be an effective leader? Let's examine the uncommon ways uncommon people became uncommon leaders.

Footprints - What is Leadership?

Ok, so we have addressed the question of what makes a leader. Now is a good time to describe what leadership really is. Remember our guy Watson. One of the primary reasons Watson was such an ineffective leader at the start of our relationship was his view of just what leadership was. He was a bottom line guy remember. His basic idea of leadership was too narrow – first to be first. Winning and profit were his primary motives. He believed that in the end all people had a basic desire to have as much in life as possible and that having much is what made them successful in all other aspects of life. But now we know that leadership is probably much more than what Watson thought it to be.

We have some fairly popular and accepted views of leadership from which we can start to reflect. Jim Collins, in the book "Good to Great" describes the level-five leader as a person who blends extreme personal humility with intense professional will. When circumstances and opportunity collide with a person of this nature great things are possible. John Maxwell defines leadership as influence, nothing more and nothing less.

So what is your idea of leadership? Take a moment to reflect on what you feel leadership is for you. Both Collins' and Maxwell's views of leadership focus on defining the impact the leader's action has on others or on an organization. When we examine the footprints of uncommon people we find something greater. I have found the uncommon leader describes leadership more as what they do in support of and for others and what they do in support of and for their organizations.

There is inherent good in the nature of uncommon leadership. It's like quality; you know it when you see it or the reverse is true. You can tell when it is missing. Uncommon people recognize this important aspect of leadership and thus they operate by a vision of leadership that considers the importance of the social orientation a leader has toward people and the operational orientation the leader carries toward achieving results. *So we describe uncommon leadership as individual effectiveness and success at achieving results, by influencing and developing the self; by influencing and developing others and by enabling others to do the same.*

I believe this description of leadership is a good place to start our discussion of what is important - to start shaping your perspective about leadership. We believe when you have an uncommon standard for leading you will be better positioned to achieve uncommon results from your leadership.

When I work with leadership teams, businesses and other organizations it is common to find that leaders on the same team view leadership in different ways. Unfortunately, I typically find this to be the root cause of many of the underlying leadership problems – leaders not aligned with leaders on just what leadership is to their organizations or leaders having unhealthy, undeveloped or immature perspectives about leading.

Recognizing Effective Leadership

"Nothing proves so conclusively a man's ability to lead others as what he does from day to day to lead himself".
Thomas J. Watson Sr.

From an economic perspective we have leading and lagging indicators that give us an idea of the health of and or direction the economy is heading. For example, the stock market is commonly viewed as a leading indicator of the strength of the economy. When stock prices rise businesses and people are encouraged and motivated to invest more. In this sense the stock market is seen as a leading indicator of an economy that is moving upward; the stock market and consumer confidence change before the economy actually changes.

Likewise unemployment is a lagging indicator. When unemployment is high it is an indication that the economy is generally not doing well; the unemployment rate will not change until there are clear changes in the economy. We can use this same idea of leading and lagging indicators to help up qualify the effectiveness of our leadership. High morale in your business would be a leading indicator that leadership is strong and effective; but a high turnover rate in your business may be a lagging indicator of weak leadership. Leading indicators are what we see first and lagging indicators are what we see as a result!

It is important to learn to recognize effective and ineffective leadership; you draw your examples and conclusions about your own leadership primarily from what you see and what you believe. Follow a poor example and you will become a poor leader.

Everyone wants to believe their leadership is good. But one of the greatest weaknesses of the common view leader is that they tend to believe everything they say to themselves about themselves. You must take care to examine what you come to believe about yourself before you believe it all. Some things you believe may not be true; some things may not be the best. This doesn't mean we should doubt ourselves - only that we should check ourselves against a better a standard and that we check constantly. Footprints will help you learn to recognize a better standard of effective leadership than your own.

John Maxell in his book "Developing the Leader within You" notes that most people have the desire to look for the exception rather than to nurture the desire to become exceptional. It is not likely we can establish ourselves as effective leaders when we choose for ourselves the quick and expedient over uncommon good for others.

I have found most people are blissfully unaware of the effectiveness of their own leadership. The immature common view leaders like to think that if they mean well, then the things they do should be received well even if things do not always turn out well. They typically judge themselves by their intents but they judge the leadership of others by their actions.

The uncommon leader is different. He uses three areas of focus as measures to ensure his leadership effectiveness is always as effective as others need it to be. I call them the three self's of leadership: self-awareness, self-assurance; and self-control.

- Self-awareness – you must know your strengths and your weakness as well as others will come to know them. You are likely to hear about both of them at some time;
- Self-assurance – you must gain confidence from your competence and from your ability to deliver results through others and;
- Self-control – you must learn to effectively manage yourself so that others do not have to manage around you. Self-control means you keep emotions, passion and desires in check before they must be checked by someone else.

Master these three areas of self and you can be more confident you are on a path to developing effective leadership.

Footprints — Chapter One — Leadership Indicators

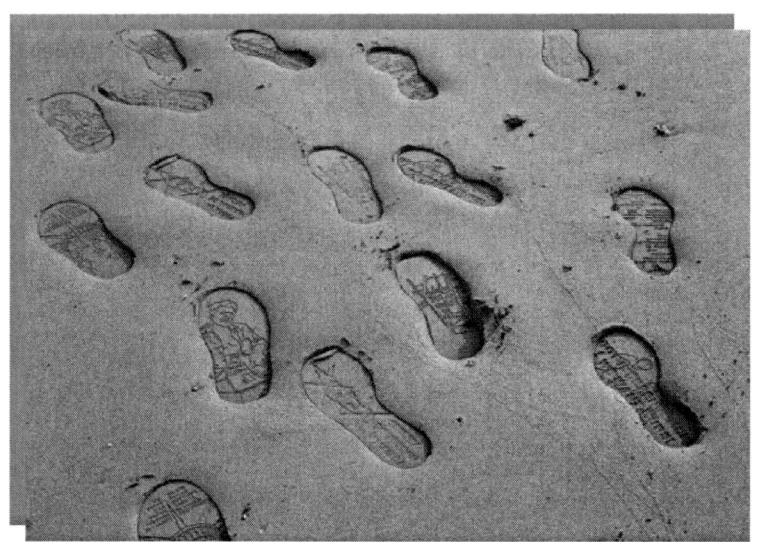

You can tell an effective leader from an ineffective leader by looking at the footprints around the leader. The footprints around an effective leader will closely match the leader's footprints. They will generally point in the same direction. They will be tightly knit together to indicate harmony and alignment. The footprints that surround an ineffective leader will be dispersed; they will often head in opposite or opposing directions; and they will indicate nonalignment with the leader.

Stages of Uncommon Development

Watson and many people like him remind me that becoming a leader means you have to be willing to take a journey that has no specific destination; a journey that has no specific no end; and one that has no defined outcome save your personal development as an effective leader. It's a journey that works to develop and perfect you in the ways you will be expected to impact the development of others.

In my own years of development, I have learned the path we take along this journey has five stages of development we must master in order to develop the uncommon leadership effectiveness we see in the uncommon people among us. These stages of development are:

- The Footprints of Maturation! First learning to be successful with you.
- The Footprints of Qualification! Becoming unquestionably qualified and competent.
- The Footprints of Collaboration! Learning to connect with others.
- The Footprints of Determination! Learning to get things done through the efforts of others.

- The Footprints of Transformation! Learning to develop leaders more than followers.

It is important that we view these stages of development as sequential steps along a journey in our development to become more effective people. Leaders are not made over night. There is no single or compelling act; no significant accomplishment; no ability to influence or to persuade others; no measure of courage or any other thing that is singularly or adequately sufficient to make you an effective leader.

In fact just as we continue to mature with time, our effectiveness as a leader is dynamic and not static – constantly evolving. Leadership development is fluid and it must remain relevant to the times and to the needs of the people and the businesses that are led. Leaders should never reach peak effectiveness. They must continue evolving throughout the different stages of life.

Until now most approaches to developing effective leadership have focused on training and activities because we are a short termed, transaction-focused world. And in our rush to achieve success we have found training and actions are easy to conduct and easy to measure; we want results and we want those results yesterday, so we are quick to seek training but slow to allow development.

It's no wonder we are this way. We require more than we inspire; we deem more than we dream and we believe the more we do the greater we become. As a result, people often incorrectly associate effective leadership too strongly with what is done by those in positions of leadership, by those with authority and or by those who have achieved results. Results are essential to becoming an effective leader but achieving results is not a shortcut to becoming a leader. This brings to mind what I have come to call "The Law of Leadership". You cannot achieve uncommon leadership effectiveness by going through a drive through window.

The journey and the path of development is the same for everyone and it cannot be shortcut by merely choosing to do some of the things leaders do; this only delays your development and your ability to be successful. It is important to be timely – if you are in a position of leadership already – the people you lead and those who lead you cannot wait years for your development. So it is important to start your journey today. It takes a little more time than you think, doing a little more work than you thought, to develop in each of us the components of leadership so that they work together in a fully complimentary way. It's time to get started!

Developing Healthy Leadership Perspectives

Uncommon views on common views about leadership

Your perspective is perhaps the most important factor that will enable or inhibit your ability to develop effective leadership. Why is this so? Well it is because it is more likely people can act out what they are able to envision within. How you view it is how you will do it. Remember our example Watson whose perspective about leadership was to be the first to be first. This may have been right for Watson alone, but he found it a difficult perspective for others to share.

I wrote Footprints after a twenty-plus year career as a military officer in our Army. I was developed to be a leader by some of our greatest military and civilian leaders. It was during that time and my times subsequently working with business leaders in the corporate world that I discovered several important things about the perspective of uncommon people who consistently deliver uncommon effectiveness.

- As it relates to success – they think and reason through second and third order impacts of all they do;
- As it relates to acts – they seek to transform more than they transact;

- As it relates to impact – the seek to become a significance more than a difference with others and in their businesses;
- As it relates to life – they seek to provide meaning and purpose for others beyond work or through work;
- As it relates to prosperity – they take responsibility for how far people advance and how far the business advance;
- As it relates to setting direction – they focus on knowing and sharing why as a function of getting to what and how and;
- As it relates to them personally – success to them is to serve the needs of others and the organizations to which they belong. They give a lot to establish their success when common leaders seek to get a lot to establish their success.

This information illustrates more clearly the importance of your perspective and the perspective of those around you.

Common Perspectives	Uncommon Perspectives
In authority	Under authority
In power	Empower
The one supported	The one who supports
In charge	Charged with
Develops others to follow	Develops others to lead
Knows what	Knows why

- When our perspective of leadership is limited to being the person in authority, we typically stand apart and restrain others but when we are under authority we stand with others and restrain ourselves;
- In power we gather to ourselves but empower we give to others and enable;
- Supported we are assisted – to support we must assist;
- In charge we overshadow others – charged with we increase others;
- Developing followers we build our stature and contribution – developing leaders we improve the contribution and value of others and;
- Knows what – we dictate priorities and steps – knows why we set direction and encourage potential.

Perspectives - Transactional to Transformational!

Today perhaps more than at during any other time greater individual leadership effectiveness is necessary for our individual and collective good. People, homes, businesses and even nations today are more issues and desires driven than purpose driven. We have developed an approach to leadership that I call common view. Common view leading happens when the people or organizations that are led generally seek and willingly support only the leadership that promises to drive and deliver a particular issue, desire or cause that is important to them. As a result leaders and developers of leaders look for cause-driven or issue-focused leadership. We have become people who generally do not want to be led; we are generally people who would rather lead those who should lead us. This is what I mean by common view leader. The leader leads to what the people or the business wants; when the leader should bring needed change to those who are led, the led are instead causing the leader to change.

Of course reasonable people know common view leadership or leading our leaders won't work for everyone if it works at all. We cannot have a common good for all and still have our individual good too. Things just don't work that way. The world is inescapably more interconnected today. We have global economies; national defense alliances; global responses to health and safety, greater racial and ethnic diversity and so on.

Whether we realize it or not; whether we are at the top or the bottom; whether we have much or have little – someone else's leadership, good or bad, has either a direct or indirect effect on each and every one of us. We may be able to live in isolation from the presence of others but we can hardly any longer live in isolation from what others do even in their own homes, cities, states or countries. I am reminded of a popular song, "I Need You to Survive", which expresses the dependent nature of the world today. Maybe we are at a point where we should say I need you to be better so I can survive.

By myself I might be able to overcome my own ineffectiveness but it is a greater challenge for me to prosper while having to overcome the ineffectiveness of others. The world has always had people who suffered from a lack of opportunity and people who have struggled to meet their basic needs for survival. People and even countries with needs for basic necessities have always been with us and they will always be among us. That's just the way it is with people and nations.

Times are seemingly more challenging today than at any time in our past. While it seems on the whole we have more today than ever before, we still seem to have less than what we need. Nations struggle with internal challenges to survive; world economies struggle with sustaining growth; and businesses around the world struggle to remain relevant. The distinction between those who have much and those who have little is becoming more blurry with each day. Though these things may seem to have come to us from nowhere, common view leadership is the one thread at the core of our problems.

Chapter Three
Sow a Thought Reap an Act

It's a critical time for people everywhere. We have become such a short-termed focused society that the way of strong effective leadership that carries the responsibility to lead others effectively has become poorly developed and in many ways seemingly unimportant to the objectives and ends we hope to achieve. When times and circumstances demand that we transform who we are and how we behave in order to achieve greater and more lasting successes, we remain steadfastly focused on doing more and greater things just as we are.

I believe it will take uncommon leadership to change our direction so that we change our outcomes. The prevailing common view leadership of the day will not change things for us in the ways they must be changed. The leader of the future must be different from the people he leads.

From Today	Establish	To The Future
Wants to succeed	Rapid learning	Refusal to accept failure
Narrow commitment	Common values	Broad commitment
Self-interest	Greater cause	Selfless interest
Externally motivated	Higher inspiration	Self-motivated
Undeveloped judgment	Evolution to new challenges	Sound judgment

Chapter Three

Sow a Thought Reap an Act

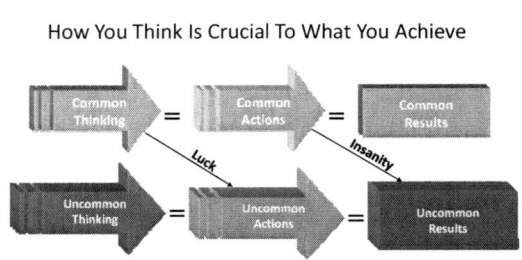

How You Think Is Crucial To What You Achieve

In October 2008, retired General and former Secretary of State Colin Powell endorsed then presidential candidate Barack Obama as the next President of the United States. Powell explained his endorsement this way. He said *I truly believe that at this point in America's history we need a president who will not just continue ... basically the policies we have followed in recent years. He said. We need a president with transformational leadership qualities. For that reason, he said, I will be voting for Barack Obama.*

I believe Powell saw the challenges the people of the United States faced and concluded that as a nation we needed more to change our ways as a function of changing our ends and objectives. And to achieve this he saw that leadership – uncommon transformational leadership – was what we needed most. In other words, we needed a transformational leader for our next president more than we needed a president with a common view of leading.

Powell's transformational leader is the opposite of the transactional leader – the two types of leaders found in current organizational theory. The transactional leader is a common view leader. The basic difference between transactional and

32

transformational leaders can have a profound impact on the success of people. The table below shows visually the impact of moving from a transactional to a transformational style of leadership.

Transactional Leader	To	Transformational Leader
Structured and rule-based	→	Adaptive and flexible
Tasked focused using people	→	People focused using tasks
Short term results	→	Solutions with strategic impact
Passive and reactive	→	Proactive and predictive
External motivation	→	Self-motivation
Problem solving	→	Creating change
Recognition for what is done	→	Acknowledgement for how things are done

It takes a lot more effort as a transactional leader to achieve results of the same level you achieved yesterday. Things all around us are evolving faster than we can adapt. In almost every segment of our society, businesses that pursue a transactional operational model are failing. They fail because their appetite for growth exceeds their ability to achieve growth in a transactional way. Transactional successes are short lived; they deplete resources; and they are difficult to repeat with any real consistency and predictability. Remember the predicament of the stallion. Each day the stallion must expend more time and energy just to keep up with where things were the day before. It is an exhausting approach to leading.

One of the most popular and most damaging ideas to develop in the business scene over the past 20 years is the transactional phrase "do more with less". The idea is supposed to motivate and encourage employees to work harder toward achieving growth objectives in difficult economic times where budget cuts and headcount reductions impact available resources. Typically this approach to business only stretches people to the point where they are even more ineffective; they are made to do lots but achieve less. The idea of doing more with less is a form of corporate dysfunction born through the common view perspective of transactional leadership.

These are some of the reasons why the leadership of every single one person matters! In order to influence the decisions and actions of the people around you – even your leaders – your effectiveness as a leader must be greater than ever. The most effective people don't wait for a particular circumstance to occur to become leaders; effective people are effective leaders because they realize they must lead at all times and in all circumstances affecting the things that will have an impact on the lives and the things of the greatest interest and importance to them.

Footprints is written to be your coach and mentor in much the same way I have been coached and mentored throughout my life and in much the same way I coach and mentor people everywhere. This is important to you because no one ever learned what it really means to be a leader by simply reading a book. The challenge is too great and it is too easy to misread the common path for the uncommon path to leading.

We are not leaders because we are better than the non-leaders around us; we are not leaders because we have talents and skills others do not have. Those who believe this way are common view leaders. We are leaders because we decide others need us to be better than we are. We start learning about and developing good leadership skills before we think about becoming your leader. Learning about leadership is what inspires us to want to become the best leader we can become. And that inspiration and determination is what enables us to rise to the level to be noticed as a potential leader.

What makes uncommon people effective also makes them stand out as leaders long before they are chosen to be leaders!

Perspectives - Rights, Authority and Responsibility!

"The exercise of power is not the same as the practice of leadership".
James MacGregor

Uncommon leaders have uncommon views on the leader's rights! I often find young people (not just young in age but young in maturity) have poor views and perspectives about leadership because of the examples they see before them. Young people may work for a leader who is a micromanager; they may know leader who is controlling and directive; they may have to collaborate with a leader who is uncooperative and self-serving. These are the examples they have of people who are seemingly successful leaders.

When I was in the Army working in my unit out in the field, I often wondered about the quality of military leaders in the Pentagon and the policies they made for the operational units in the field. Then one day I was assigned to the Pentagon in a role where I had to make the policies for units in the field. I was determined never to use my authority and rank as a high ranking official to direct what the units needed to do because that did not create a collaborative healthy relationship between me and the units.

I learned that demanding my rights and exercising authority were the least effective ways to interface with and influence others. Power, rights and authority come with the role or a position; it can be used to get people to do things but it can come and go easily. And the more you use these tools with people the more you will need to continue to use them on people. Funny thing too – the more you rely on your rights, authority and power the more people are inclined to act within their rights and authority and power.

I think I heard John Maxwell say people will rise or sink to the level of your leadership. I agree with that. The more rights focused the leader is the more self-focused people will be. In the end your effectiveness as a leader must be derived more from your disposition than from your position. Rights, authority, power and so forth cannot give you the influence, commitment and the hearts of people. You can only earn that. In all my years of military service it was commonly understood that the most effective military leaders learned that the responsibility to lead is a far more useful tool for achieving results through others than relying on the right to lead.

When I was promoted to Captain in the Army, I thought there was no one greater than me. I set out the next day to make sure that every person subordinate to me in rank gave me the respect I was due. I was something – or so I thought! One day a sergeant, someone subordinate to me, was wise enough and cared enough to take me aside and enlighten me on what it meant to lead with an uncommon perspective.

He said *Captain every soldier here will respect your rank because that is what the Army requires. But I cannot see any soldier ever growing to respect and honor you until you learn to get past your rank and you allow the soldiers to do so as well.* If you grow up to be full of pride about yourself and the position you hold as a leader, those you lead are likely to become full of you too. I learned that effectiveness ultimately must come from the person you are as a leader and not the position, not authority or not even the experience you have attained. Noted author Kenneth Blanchard says it this way, *the key to successful leadership today is influence, not authority.*

Perspectives - Learning to Achieve Results!

It isn't fair to say leadership is all for naught if you don't achieve results, but likewise it would be naïve to say results do not matter as long as you lead well. Results matter but they just do not matter the most. The uncommon leaders have uncommon views on getting things done. They describe leadership as focused on results because they recognize that some people do not always carry through to the end what needs to be done to be successful. Why then do some organizations create and sustain winning success while others lag in mediocrity? Noel Tichy and Eli Cohen, in their book "The Leadership Engine" say *winning organizations win because they have good leaders who nurture the development of other leaders at all levels of the organization...the ultimate test of a leader is not whether he or she makes smart decisions and takes decisive action, but whether he or she teaches others to be leaders and builds an organization that can sustain its success when the leader is not present.*

It is your responsibility as a leader to teach others how to be successful. Too often leaders overlook this simple but critical dimension to effectiveness. Often time people know what to do but they do not necessarily know how to be successful. Uncommon leaders take the time to develop their greatest competence in three areas critical to creating and perpetuating results. They learn to create incremental results no matter how small; they learn to work for and achieve the commitment of others and; they learn to develop

Footprints   Chapter Three   Results Through
The Efforts of Others

The organization's strength beyond where it was yesterday. I call these the components of success.

The key component in this model is earning the commitment of others. Uncommon leaders stand out in the ability to earn the commitment of the people they lead. And as they earn commitment they use this commitment to make the organization stronger. As they make the organization stronger they are then able to help the organization achieve more and greater organizational

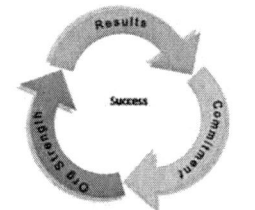
Success Model – Perpetuating Results

results. As the organization achieves greater results people will then give them more of their commitment – they dig into their potential.

And so the perpetual motion of results and commitment and organizational strength begins to work. Results or winning inspires people – the uncommon leader learns how to get things done through the efforts of others; commitment binds people – the uncommon leader learns to gain the commitment of others more than looking for the obedience of others. Building organizational strength motivates people – the uncommon leader learns to build organizational capability by using people productively. We will talk more about commitment and results when we get to the detail of each stage of our development as a leader of uncommon effectiveness. But for now it is important to understand that results don't just happen by chance.

There is a method and a process by which consistent results are achieved. The people you lead must believe that you know how to achieve results in the most efficient way or they will work to their limits rather than to their potential. I have consulted with leaders of many organizations and I have not found one yet who has achieved and sustained success when its people simply come in and do an honest day's work. The people of winning organizations typically must do more than what is required by the job.

Remember that people cannot rise above the limits of your leadership. The more effective you are the more effective they will be; the weaker you are the weaker you make them. Mediocre people will stay with a weak leader because it is safe; but competent people will leave a weak leader because they will feel held back. All leaders derive their effectiveness from one of three places: their position, their experience and their person. The least most effective of these is the position. The most desirable of these is the person. Let me illustrate this point.

The Source of Leadership Effectiveness

Position Derived	Experience Derived	Person Derived
Task/Activity Focused	Mission / Operations Focused	Strategic / Institution Focused
Leads Projects / Programs	Develops Projects / Programs	Develops Institutions
Solves Problems	Anticipates Identifies Problems	Transforms Problems
Drives Productivity	Improves Capability	Creates Capability
Directs / Motivates	Guides, Influences and Inspires	Inspires, Coaches and Develops
Relies on Position and Authority	Relies on Aptitude, Influence and Trust	Relies on value of others
Transactional Potential	Transformational Potential	Transformational Potential

I find far too many leaders rely too much on position derived effectiveness. As a result they struggle to achieve and maintain a consistent level of successful growth. The approach is far too short term focused and too reactive. When I first met him, Watson used this approach almost exclusively. When you view the table from left to right you can see the natural progression of effectiveness. The person who derives effectiveness primarily from the position will struggle when it's required to lead more based on the experiences you have or the person you are. The footprints of uncommon leaders show a natural development and progression from position

Chapter Three

derived through experienced derived to person derived effectiveness.

This is important because whether you lead in a personal setting like your home and family or whether you lead yourself as part of a business or whether you are leader of a business, the world is not designed to sit by and enable you to enjoy unimpeded success. When I work with a business to develop their strategic plans or the plans for their future, I am always careful to point out the challenges the business must overcome to achieve and maintain the success they seek.

There are six challenges to sustaining consistent success I find that occur repeatedly in almost every business or organization or with any person. They are:

- Having a planning horizon that is far too short – expecting long term success from short term initiatives;
- Failing to secure buy-in throughout the organization – 20% of the people shoulder 80% of the critical work;
- Focusing more on what to do than where to go – losing sight of the objective while busy reading the map;
- Misalignment of making plans; making decisions and executing – working on what wasn't planned and planning what is not worked;
- Unclear direction and destination – clear direction that causes confusion and;

Chapter Three

- Leadership effectiveness that fit yesterday's needs not tomorrow's objectives – what got us here will get us there.

Achieving results is about getting results! Watson would be happy to hear that. But achieving results tomorrow is progressively more difficult than what you do today. Effectiveness of the leader must be progressive. Achieving results is about setting clear direction for others; creating processes for people that are scalable and repeatable; developing excellence and earning identification for being the "best" at something. Getting results includes investing in making people better than they are today; making wise timely decisions and; developing personal accountability and responsibility for your actions and the actions of those you lead.

The uncommon leader teaches others how to execute effectively. They develop environments so that people either work within process to gain efficiencies with current capabilities or they work with processes to learn and to execute beyond their potential. Said another way, people either know what they are doing and are increasing efficiencies or they are learning to expand the impact of their contribution through a process the leader develops.

Efficiency and Potential

When efficiency is the point	When learning is the point
Leaders provide answers	Leaders set direction and articulate the mission
Others follow directions	Others discover the way
Processes are designed in advance	Processes are starting points not ends
Feedback is one way – leader down	Two way feedback is common
People rarely make judgment calls	People continually make important judgment calls

Let me offer a final word on your perspective about leadership. The challenge for us is to develop a healthy perspective of leadership and to act it out. Because Watson initially had a very narrow perspective of leading, the people around him groaned at the ineffectiveness of his idea of leadership. So we must take care never to believe all that we tell ourselves about our leadership. Watson made major changes in how he views and acts out his leadership and as a result today his people produce more than ever primarily because they do not find his leadership intolerable any longer. A healthy perspective will be characterized by the leader who considers the importance of:

- Learning that success with the self is a precondition for success with others;

Chapter Three

- Learning to solve problems quickly by first looking within the self;
- Learning to understand human nature – especially their own;
- Learning to mature faster than they age and;
- Learning to gauge and to overcome the negative impact they have on others.

Perspectives - The Promise!
A case illustration demonstrating uncommon perspectives on leading!
Footprints

You are the leader of a small team of professionals. A member of your team, someone you have known for several years, comes to you and says, *I overhead something today from someone on our team about our project that if true it could have a terrible impact on those of us working on the project. I think you should know what this person said but before I tell you about it you must promise me you will not tell anyone I'm the one who told you this.*

How do you respond to this person? See the next page for my explanation.

The Promise Explained

So how would you respond? Well I've found the uncommon leaders typically never make that promise. In fact they never even give the idea serious consideration. They do not make this promise because as a leader they would themselves never ask that such a promise be made; leaders just don't do that. Let me explain that statement.

The uncommon leader is always working to develop leaders of others. They know that the relationship between the leader and those they led must have a foundation of trust. The people you lead must trust you to act in the best overall interest of all at all times. By asking for this promise the person led is saying in one sense my fears for myself keep me from trusting you to act in a way that will be to my best interest.

A leader should never allow fear, anxiety or personal concerns to cloud the need for them to make the hard right decisions. Remember I said people cannot rise above the level of your leadership. When you allow fear and things such as this to affect your leadership you are limited and so are the people you lead.

In this instance the uncommon leader does not make this promise because the leader would be limited by the undeveloped and immature person they lead. Well now at this point in my seminars some people would say to me suppose this information is life threatening! Suppose this information is detrimental to the company! Suppose! Suppose! Suppose! Yes, the information could be anything and it could be nothing. But to get at the information a leader never make deals such as this. Once you as a leader start to allow others to lead you because of their fears or weaknesses it will be difficult for you to lead them effectively in almost any other area.

I have found today that the voices of those led can be so great sometimes that they tend to change the leader when it is the leader who should most often change and transform others. The uncommon leader does several things in instances like this that are uniquely effective and uncommon. They typically get the information and more. They focus on teaching the person to:

- Think the way a leader would think (I'm responsible to act on what I know);
- Behave like a leader (this is what a leader must do);
- Achieve like a leader (this is how a leader gets results);
- See like a leader (there are more important issues here than what I am seeing and);
- Build like a leader (I must strengthen the weak links in others in order to make them stronger parts of the team).

Remember, the leader has an operational responsibility toward the business, organization, team etc., to ensure things work as they should. But there is always the social responsibility the leader has toward developing the people of the business to make better life choices. Leaders of uncommon effectiveness do not see this as an either or situation. Through their actions mature leaders confirm that people are the business and the business is about people.

Our description of leadership balances the responsibility the leader has toward people and the need to accomplish things. But maturity and development of this nature takes time, commitment and patience. It takes time to learn how to develop your leadership potential and effectiveness; it takes commitment and practice to prepare yourself to achieve results from what you know and learn about leadership and; it takes patience to see your commitment manifested in practical and experiential effectiveness.

Preparing for Leadership

"If I had eight hours to cut down a tree, I would spend six hours sharpening my axe".
Abraham Lincoln

For the many years now I have conducted executive leadership development seminars, I continue to find one common challenge. Most people come to my seminars having devoted most of their lives to trying to make a train car perspective of life work more successfully.

By that I mean they decide early in life what they want to do or become – this becomes the engine of their train. Then they spend the rest of their lives adding cars to their engine. First they add the car that contains what they need to know; then they add the car that contains what they need to do; and finally they add the cars that contain the desires of their lives. The problem with this approach to life is preparation. People usually find the engine they start with is not prepared to pull all the cars they end with.

During each seminar I typically ask each person *where or when did you learn to become the leader you are today?* The question usually draws blank stares and empty responses. Most people can remember the time and place when they made the conscious decisions to pursue their current skill, work or profession.

Chapter Four — Sharpening The Axe

Preparation should be so uncommon it never ends! A dull axe will do more harm than good.

But very few if any, can ever recall a point in life where they made a conscious decision to become a leader.

Abraham Lincoln is quoted to have said *if I had eight hours to cut down a tree, I would spend six hours sharpening my axe.* This insight gives us an incredible perspective on the value of taking time to prepare for the challenges we will face. Your leadership is the single most important determinant of the level of personal or professional success you can ever achieve in your lifetime and beyond. Your development as a leader starts when you commit to meeting the challenge of preparing yourself to be successful with yourself and with the talents and skills you will acquire in your life.

Most people often stop working on themselves too soon and they start working on others too quickly.

Development is the time you take to sharpen the axe of your life before you put your life to work. Skills and talent alone are not enough to bring about long term consistent success. Long before your skills as a leader are put to the tree, your life as a leader must be sharpened.

Think about the areas of your life that must be sharpened today in order to prepare you to be a more effective leader tomorrow? In my work as a leader in working to develop the leadership effectiveness of others, I have discovered three areas or dimensions of leadership that must be sharpened to accelerate the development of a leader's effectiveness. These dimensions are:

- Personal – understanding who you must BE as a leader;
- Social – understanding what you must KNOW as a leader and;
- Professional – understanding what you must DO as a leader.

The personal dimension of who you must BE answers the question who are you? Consider what are the five most important qualities of a leader? Most people will include things such as honesty, truthfulness, a person of character, integrity and so on. These are qualities of the person you ARE and not of what you do. The seeds for developing the qualities that shape our personal BE dimension are set within each of us early. But they must be developed so they are perfected.

Too often we pay little to no attention to them; we think that who we are is ultimately the end result of a natural course of development that comes as we learn what we want to do with our God given talents and skills. This is wrong. Who we are does not follow what we come to do in life; who we are forms the foundation of all that we can know and do well in life. It is where we all begin – not end.

Each of us who are parents should understand the BE dimension of development well. Even before a child is able to walk or talk they begin to form the footprints of who they are; we typically describe a child using BE descriptors more than anything else. The challenge for us is to decide to continue to work on who we must BE throughout our lives.

Trust is settled in who we are and it comes in two ways. People will learn to trust in us for what we do because they have settled to trust us for who we are. We are not naturally people of integrity; integrity is something we must develop. We are not naturally people of honesty; honesty is something we must develop. We are not naturally selfless people; selflessness is something we must develop ourselves to be. Each of these traits are things people – especially leaders, ARE; they are developmental areas that sustain the Social (KNOW) and Professional (DO) dimensions of people or leaders.

The social dimension of what you KNOW answers the question what you must KNOW as a person or leader? It is an area that can be learned – cognitive. Learning happens from the experiences of life. We must be willing to educate and to develop ourselves to always learn not for ourselves but for others. The train car that represents what we have learned should be filled to a capacity greater than the level of what we need to know today. A leader doesn't have to know everything but he should know what he ought to know or he should know how to learn it.

Again if we asked about important leadership qualities many of us would include things such as knowledgeable; knows what to do; is experienced and so forth. The point to make about the KNOW dimension of leadership is simple; every leader should feel as if they are lifelong learners because the people and the businesses we lead need us to be more knowledgeable for them than for ourselves.

Let me caution you here. Knowledge is not an indication of intelligence or of how smart we are. The mastery of learning and expanding what we KNOW is however an indication of whether others will trust us; whether others will have confidence in us; and whether others will believe in us. It is a major factor in how others will view us.

The professional dimension of what you DO answers the question what you must DO as a person or leader? What we do is more behavioral; it is an area where we must be trained to bring change and to improve effectiveness. A poorly trained leader is likely to be a poor performing leader.

In 2010, I worked with over 100 executive and high performing leaders. I found a consistent and disturbing trend in all those who had experienced a degree of personal or professional failure in the past; most leaders often stopped working on themselves too soon and they started working on others too quickly. I heard this quote once by someone else. *We should never stop trying to become qualified to do our jobs.* It's the point I want to make about what we DO as leaders.

Training is supposed to indicate what you are capable of doing and the level of proficiency you have achieved. However, too often we live life at such a pace that we hardly take time to train ourselves to be great at the things we do daily. I find many leaders are untrained and are learning on the go.

Many people and businesses fail because they do not find time away from their work to perfect what they must do when they are at work. The professional dimension of what we DO as leaders is where excellence, quality and perfection are established. People will come to believe in you and to commit to you when they can see that you are trained to be successful. When they believe in the quality of what you are able to do they will give more of their potential to the ideas you have for what you want to accomplish.

This model shows the relationship between the three dimensions of your leadership.

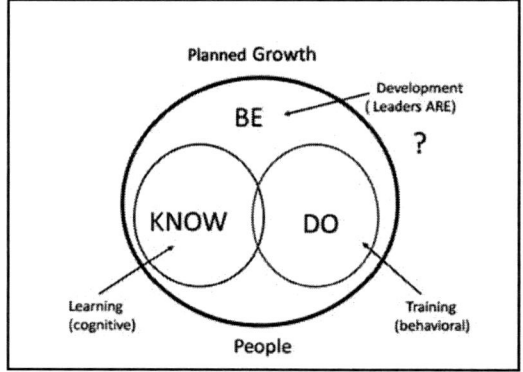

Remember, the personal dimension of who you must BE is your foundation. We are developing a strong "Who We Are". The social dimension of what you KNOW is where you develop how you will be viewed by others and the degree to which you know yourself and whether you seek self-improvement. Finally the professional dimension of what you must DO is where you spend the time to perfect what you are able to do so that you demonstrate unquestionable competence in yourself and in the people around you.

These dimensions of leadership have a strong relationship with Daniel Goleman's five components of Emotional Intelligence. The information below illustrates what I mean.

Dimensions of Leadership

Personal – BE	Social – KNOW	Professional – DO
Self-awareness	Social Skill	Motivation
Self-Regulation	Empathy	
Empathy		

When we consider the footprints of the uncommon leaders among us we find people who have realized how to use the challenges they face daily to sharpen the personal, social and professional dimensions of how they lead. Mastering these dimensions of leadership helps to ensure that you start your development with the right foot forward; that you take the right path; that you do the right things; that you end in the right place and that you achieve the right results.

The Nature and Work of Development!
An uncommon approach to development

I have learned that many people and most companies do not understand the difference between the nature of development and the objective of training. It's a fine line of differentiation but it has profound impacts on the effectiveness and abilities of leaders and people in general to perform to higher levels.

Your development as a leader must be viewed as a deliberate, continuous, sequential and progressive process. Development is properly done when it is experienced; it works to transform you from who you are to who you must become. Footprints is written to be a development tool; it is will allow you to experience the process of developing effective leadership by challenging who you are and what you know about yourself today.

Training on the other hand is different; training is received. People receive training to perfect skills they may or may not have. Sharpening the axe is a skill that can be trained; but having the wisdom and insight to know that a sharp axe will make the job easier is the result of the development of your nature and your experiences over time. This is why it is important that you allow your development as a leader to have its season of sharpening in your life. This information illustrates more fully the nature of development as it relates to training.

The Development / Training Contrast

Development – you become	Training – you master
A well-spoken person	Effective communication
A visionary	Creating vision
A decisive person	Improve decision making
A person of integrity	Dealing with integrity issues
A person of value to others	Creating impact and value
A leader	Things leaders must do

Among Learning and Development professionals it is commonly understood that we are able to train skills but we must grow leaders. In developing your effectiveness as a leader, values matter; influence matters; decisiveness matter; humility matters; integrity matters; results matter; all these and many more things like them matter in developing yourself to be an effectiveness leader. But what matters most is the approach you take to development.

Development is comprehensive and should include training; but training is narrowly focused and should never be thought to include development. Development will enable you to synthesize experiences, knowledge, skills and facts in such a way so as to develop in you to the ability to respond and or to act appropriately with seeming first-hand experience to things you have not yet seen.

The uncommon leader follows a clearly defined and never ending approach to self-development and development of others. The work of development should leave you feeling complete –

lacking nothing. To illustrate the nature of development and training, I often ask those who attend my development seminars to choose one of the following two statements that best describe how they feel about themselves:

- I get along with others or;
- Others get alone with me.

There is no right or wrong response. The persons who say they get along with others have probably trained themselves to work with people – even those who are difficult to be around. These people generally get along with others by training themselves to let difficult people be difficult people. They tolerate and move on for their own benefit.

The persons who say others get along with them have probably developed themselves to be positive people of value in any relationship; these people both get along with others and others get along with them. They have probably developed the ability to transform the difficult person to a more collaborative person we all need them to be.

Consider the statements again. Which are you? Don't let me fool you. You need the ability to both get along and to have others get along with you. Getting along with others is something we can train ourselves to do; but being someone others get along with is perhaps something we must develop ourselves to be.

Imperatives that Drive the Uncommon Leader!

When I work with companies I often stumble over a dichotomy of views on the priority of what a leader is supposed to do daily. If I ask a leadership team they typically say direct and guide the workforce. I generally find people in non-leadership positions have a difficult time knowing what leaders should do because they believe leaders typically focus too much on the worker's job than the leader's job.

Leaders have a job to do but it does not include doing the jobs of those they lead; this is commonly micromanagement and or controlling behavior. Uncommon leaders typically choose to play a role more than work a job. This perspective helps keep the uncommon leader focused on leader imperatives that develop and transform rather than on doing the jobs others are hired to do.

In 2010, I collaborated with leaders from the Army War College in Carlisle, Pennsylvania, on writing Footprints. The Army War College is the where the Army develops and implements all its leadership develop programs for senior military and civilians across the Department of Defense. The leaders there are uncommon people among uncommon people. They wrote the book on leadership. During my visit I found they shared an uncommon view and perspective about the things most important for leaders to do and to do well. I call these now the three imperatives of leadership.

These are:
- To develop talented people and to teach them how to be successful;
- To plan and set direction and;
- To strengthen the organization.

Developing Talented People

By developing talented people and teaching them how to be successful uncommon leaders try to increase productivity of others by increasing the value and capability of others. I worked with the CEO of a very large manufacturing company for three years. Our focus was to develop a more talented workforce for the future. This CEO had a very simple but profound view on talent, capability and productivity as they impact the success of others. He saw talent and capability as a joint responsibility between his people and the organization. The business would always hold itself accountable for working with and investing in enhancing the talents and capability of its people.

Once resourced properly, he saw productivity as an individual responsibility and accountability. Individuals had to have the desire to produce to the level of their talents and their capabilities. The role of the leader in this scenario was to keep capability and productivity in balance. As long as this happened people learned how to be consistently successful.

To reinforce the importance of keeping a balance between what people are capable of producing and what people can produce this CEO used the fable of the goose that laid the golden egg with all leaders – especially leaders new to the business. You probably know the fable – but I'll share it here with some modifications to emphasize the insight I want you to learn.

The farmer goes out to collect eggs from the goose each day. On this particular day the farmer notices the egg is discolored – it appears somewhat golden. It's also heavier than usual. Thinking the goose is just sick he puts the egg away and waits for the sickness to pass. The next day he collects yet another golden egg. After doing this for a week or so the farmer begins to think the goose may actually be laying eggs that are much more valuable than he thought. So he takes the basket of eggs in to a friend who appraised them. The friend tells the farmer what the farmer already believes – the goose is in fact laying golden eggs.

For the next two weeks the farmer takes a new basket full of eggs in to his friend for appraisal. One day his friend says to the farmer *you are old, why don't you start a business and take it public that way you can amass your wealth quickly before you die.* The farmer thinks that is a good idea so he does so. Two weeks after going public the new shareholders and board members in the business ask the farmer to increase production of golden eggs from one per day to three per day. The farmer thinks they must want their wealth too – but not just before they die but while they are young.

The next day the farmer says to the goose *you must produce three eggs per day starting tomorrow.* The goose however tells the farmer he is only capable of producing one egg per day. This goes on for a week and during this week the pressure for increased production from the farmer's board and shareholder grows. Each day the farmer reminds the goose of the new requirement and each day the goose says one per day is his capability.

When the pressure to increase production finally wears the farmer down he decides the best thing to do is to simply kill the goose and take all the eggs at one time. So the next morning after collecting still again a single golden egg the farmer takes his knife, kills and guts the goose only to find there are no more eggs to be had. The goose it seems was right – he was only capable of producing one golden egg per day.

As a leader you will need to react at times to what is above the surface – in this case the call for increased productivity. But you must be driven and you must be guided by what is below the surface where capability and strength and wisdom and insight are sown! I learned from the CEO of this manufacturing company that uncommon leaders will invest the time to develop talented people and to teach them how to be consistently successful. They develop uncommonly talented people who learn to keep capability and productivity requirements in balance but the immature leader will often unwisely destroy capability in an effort to unsuccessfully increase productivity.

Chapter Four

Planning and Setting Direction

In planning and setting direction leaders are expected to create the vision for what is possible; the mission for what should be done and set the goals for what will be done. In 2009, I led the executive team of a retail products company through a strategic planning process for the business. Their overall objective heading into our planning session was to grow the revenue of the business by a 35% increase over a five year period.

The uncommon leader knows the importance of planning. He knows that goals are good for measuring the productivity of the people; they occupy the actions of the people. But plans are necessary for showing people where the business is going; they touch the hearts of people giving them a visual of what the business can become. In knowing and showing the way, leaders enable others to have confidence in and to believe in the potential for future successes. They see the big picture!

Strengthening the Organization

In strengthening the organization uncommon leaders know they must exercise the organization in the areas where it must be stronger tomorrow than it is today. They make it stronger not bigger. They create purpose and meaning for the business and they help develop the business competence for what it can do better than any other business. Business competence is critical to differentiating one business from another. Both Dell and HP are in the business of making laptop computers. Each has that skill. But which is best? Which is the leader?

Skills identify you from those who cannot do what you do; but competencies identify you as the best among those who can. It is imperative that as a leader you understand that among all the things you must do daily these three imperatives are the tips of the spear of the competencies you will need to be consistently great; they are the tipping point to a leader's success. When taken together they speak this way. We have talented successful leaders who know the way to get to where we are going and who make our business greater by making our organization stronger.

Competencies–The Catalysts of a Leader's Effectiveness!

"Leadership skills set you apart from those who can't; leadership competencies set you above those who can". Footprints

Perhaps the question is not what is it that leaders do but what areas of competence separate the great leader from the good leader? We believe among those who are leaders, great leadership is set apart by those who:

- Effectively clarify purpose and set direction;
- Effectively create environments of collaboration and teamwork;
- Effectively transform people and the business;
- Effectively introduce change within the business;
- Effectively maintain the health of organization by dealing with conflict;
- Effectively translates leadership into the know-how to get things done.

Purpose and direction are essential to keeping people aligned and focused in the same direction especially when rules and policies are made by some for others to follow. Purpose and direction are not the same as stating the mission and setting goals. Mission is what you say you should be doing; goals describe what you commit to do in the short term. Neither provides the necessary innate sense of direction and meaning derived from purpose and direction cast by the uncommon leader.

Teamwork, change and conflict are three things that can work in opposition to one another and to your desired objectives.

Teamwork in one instance is undesired competition in others; one person's desire for change creates for another person an area of conflict; and conflict to some is growth and maturity while to others it is healthy ingredients to teamwork. Some of the most effective leaders distinguish themselves from other leaders by being very competent in creating teamwork that is best for all; driving change that is endorsed by all; and by dealing with conflict in ways that is healthy for all.

Direction, purpose, teamwork, change and transformation are necessary to effectively deal with conflict; these things help the leader clarify what is right and what is best. This is especially important for people who see right and best as a function of the authority of a particular person or in a role. They believe people (usually themselves) are right in what they say and do because it is inherent in their authority and their roles. They have an immature selfish view that what is right and appropriate or best must be inherent to the leader.

Uncommon Development Below The Surface

"Sow a thought you reap an act;
Sow an act and you reap a habit;
Sow a habit and you reap a character and;
Sow a character and you reap a destiny".
Unknown

Uncommon habits that drive uncommon behaviors

Each year since 2005, I have conducted an Executive Roundtable discussion in which leaders from the companies I have consulted with the previous year are invited to an end of the year discussion of things learned and challenges overcome. I try to create an environment where leaders can learn from one another the things that work best in developing people and in business success.

During these discussions I typically come away with new insight that can be shared the next year with new clients. I have captured what I believe are the uncommon ways great leaders use common tools to create environments where people and businesses are developed to live and operate with a view toward reaping a destiny more than for the benefit of the moment. The uncommon leader:

- Starts with and demonstrate a solid foundation from which all their actions are driven;

- Creates environments to support what they want leaders to BE;
- Develops others to be leaders more than followers;
- Uses communication to develop and inform;
- Develops vision to inspire and;
- Lead's always and manages as needed.

I call these the uncommon ways of the uncommon leader. Their ways remind me of a line from the movie Gladiator when the Roman Army General says to his soldiers before what they hope to be the last battle before world peace is achieved. He says, *Brothers what we do in life echoes in eternity!* World peace may not be at our fingertips but lasting impact that shapes the destiny of people and business is. And as the uncommon leader travels the journey that has no destination along the path that has no end, these distinctive ways are the tools used to enrich the experiences encountered along the way.

An Uncommon Foundation

The uncommon leader understands that a strong foundation is necessary to support what people and business want to be and do. They take time to identify and to develop the professional ethics, professional competencies and the guiding principles that will be the filters through which all actions of the people and the business flow.

Loyalty, integrity, selflessness, honesty, character, sound judgment, personal accountability and acquiring new knowledge and so on are a few of the pillars of ethics and competencies that all leaders are expected to live. The US Army Military Academy at West Point NY takes the position that all officers must be leaders of character and if a person does not have character that person cannot be a leader at all.

Great leaders use ethics to help determine if you can learn to overcome challenges to your growth and development. A little dishonesty may be acceptable to some people and to some organizations but to the uncommon leader a little dishonesty represents a step backwards in growth and development. The leader of uncommon significance knows that it is vitally important to distinguish between the things you or your business value and the values to which you hold yourself accountable.

I am reminded of the leader from a manufacturing business with whom I worked in 2008, to align the leaders of the business to the business value system. After a number of failed attempts to get leaders of the business to demonstrate the company's values the CEO turned to me in frustration and asked *what am I doing wrong?*

After some time assessing the problem I found it wasn't an issue of alignment – people knew and understood the company's values – rather it was accountability. People simply were not personally accountable for living the values and they found it somewhat hypocritical to try and hold another person responsible for something they did not do themselves.

We helped the CEO create an environment where each individual was expected to hold themselves personally accountable for living the business values. When there was a breach in the value system – no matter how large or small – the person was asked three questions:

- What went wrong? Did they understand what the problem was;
- What corrective action would they take with themselves to ensure the problem didn't happen again and;
- What disciplinary action, if any, would they recommend for themselves?

This approach to building a strong foundation in the business allowed the CEO to use the problem, repeated breaches of the company's values, as the tool to develop an environment of personal and professional accountability and responsibility across the company. Today everyone in this business operates in a highly accountable way because the environment requires immediate corrective action when there is a breach in behavior.

Chapter Five

The Uncommon Way Others Are Viewed

"Uncommon leaders produce better leaders because they see all people as leaders"!
Footprints

People today are a greater challenge to lead and to develop than at any time before. Great leaders tell me because so many leaders today stand out for the mistakes they make more than for the greatness they achieve, people have developed a general sense of apathy toward leadership.

To counter apathy, uncommon leaders view everyone as a leader and they develop others to be leaders more than followers. By developing each person in the organization to be a leader you can reproduce in all people the same attributes you find in successful leaders. And you are able to meet the challenge you have with people to move others from an undesirable state today; to achieve a future state for each person; and to sustain a desired outcome. The information below illustrates more fully what I mean.

The Challenge of Developing People

From Today	To the Future	To Sustain
Weak Foundations	Common Values	Commitment / Alignment
Weak Commitment	Individual Buy-in	Refusal to Fail
Leader Apathy	Self-leadership	Sustained Growth
Undeveloped Judgment	Trusted and Wise Decision Making	Transformational Impact
Low Motivation	Self-Inspired	Uncommon Results

Chapter Five

The uncommon leader believes that every person has or must have what it takes to be an effective leader; there are no places in the future for people who do not want to take the responsibility to lead themselves effectively.

This reminds me of a US Civil War General from the North whose unit defeated and captured a unit of Confederate soldiers. A Union Army Commander was charged with the responsibility to transport the prisoners to the next post. He told his Brigade Commander, *but we ourselves are depleted of resources. We have no soldiers to devote to the requirement to guarding the prisoners.*

The Union Army Brigade Commander went to the prisoners and said, *we are taking you back to the next post where you will be processed and probably released to head back to your homes. We have no followers here; now that you are with our unit we expect you to lead yourselves and do what you will be told to do; so long as you do this we will treat you like we treat all leaders in our unit.*

The prisoners understood what the General meant. They were not guarded at all during the march back to the post. No prisoner attempted to escape nor did anyone cause any problem for the union command. Uncommon leaders have learned that if you treat others as leaders they will likely respond like leaders.

Why did this work with for the Army Unit? Because the Army then, as it does now, places an emphasis on developing people first to be leaders and then giving those leaders responsibility for a job. It is a challenge – not insurmountable for others because the emphasis is not the same. This table illustrates the emphasis of leadership in different sectors of our society. You could add your home, church, government or almost any other environment to the table. There are strengths and weaknesses in each sector. But there is a common core – the way you sustain leadership is to grow leadership.

Leadership Focus by Sector

Emphasis	Military	Political	Business
Essence	First the leader then the role	First the ideology then the people	First the role then the person
Sustaining Leadership	Growing leaders and training skills	Preserving the organization by appealing to people	Training people on leadership skills
Focus on Results	Improving the capability of others	Improving the opportunities for others	Increasing the productivity and output of others
Emphasis on Tasks	Why and how things are done	Which things align with the mass	Who and what things are done
Leadership / Management	Lead first then manage	Respect leadership and critique management	Manage first then lead
Leader's Core Purpose	Establish purpose and direction for others	Establish environment for others to live	Establish goals and objectives for what others must do

Chapter Five
Seeing Leaders Not Followers

    The uncommon leader approaches development in an uncommon way. Leaders develop others to be leaders; they accept no followers in their businesses; they accept no followers in their homes; they accept no followers on their teams. Everyone is expected to demonstrate, live and be accountable to the things that all leaders must do to lead the first person well – themselves.

An Uncommon Use of Communication

"Wise men talk because they have something to say; fools, because they have to say something".
Plato

There is perhaps no aspect of effective leadership that gets more attention than the need to communicate more effectively. There are books written on this topic alone; there are businesses designed to focus on nothing more than helping you to become more effective at communication. Human nature is a powerful thing. It has a great way of knowing when a person says one thing but the heart wants another; it has a great way of knowing when a person says a lot but leaves a lot to be said and; it has a great way of knowing a person is as confused about what to say as the hearer is about what is heard.

During week of my first assignment as a Second Lieutenant in the Army my boss asked me to come to his office. He handed me an Army award. The award is pretty standard; they are limited to 13 lines with the first two lines and the last two lines being a standard introduction and closing words for all awards across the Army. My boss then asked me to read the award out loud. Now he and I were the only two people in his office so I thought he was a little crazy to ask me to do that but I complied. After finishing he took the award and said, *good job. Now do you understand what this all means? I told him I thought it meant I should practice reading awards because he may ask me to do that again sometime in the future.* He said *no you misunderstand. I am asking you what all these words mean, gesturing to the award.* He made a deliberately ambiguous statement in order to make a point about communication and to learn something about me.

Here was my lesson about communication. He told me great leaders have uncommon ways of communicating so that they learn from others and learn about others. People receive what is said in one of two basic ways. They either reason what was said by asking questions and then walking through what was said to arrive at their understanding or they rationalize what they hear and look only for the evidence in what was said to support what they believe they heard. The way my boss communicated his question was clear to him but confusing to me; so I rationalized what I thought I he meant and then looked for the evidence in what he said to support what I thought he meant. I didn't ask him a clarifying question before I offered my response to his question. My boss wanted to know if I were one who would reason through ambiguity or rationalize my reality. I missed the point of what he wanted me to learn but he learned something incredibly valuable about me. I needed to learn to reason more and to rationalize less.

I learned from that experience and from many years writing for very senior military and Department of Defense Officials and from conducting executive development seminars all over the world that effective communication is the responsibility of the leader. As complex and as comprehensive the act *Communicate in a way so that you teach others how to communicate more effectively!*

of communication is, the uncommon leader knows that he speaks to people who will either reason or rationalize what is said. So he must be very clear.

Uncommon leaders want to develop people who learn to reason more effectively and to rationalize less. The way they do this is through effective use of communication. And though the leader's self-awareness, confidence, passion, knowledge, message and style are all important components of the overall communication process, they do three things that set them apart for the way they communicate:

- Transparency and clarity are imperative! First the leader learns to be clear and concise in oral communication. This means the leader must eliminate as much as possible the possibility of multiple meanings in the message;
- Think about their thinking! Second the leader takes time to reason through what is to be said to determine if the conclusion reached is the one desired and;
- Listen twice as much as they speak! Third the leader becomes one who says only what has to be said and never one who speaks because they just have to say something.

Dale Carnegie is quoted to have said *speak clearly if you speak at all; carve every word before you let it fall.* People who use communication to develop how others communicate as much as they do to inform others usually learn to be more effective communicators.

Let me offer you a small tip here on how you can start yourself on the journey to communicate more effectively. Uncommon leaders do three things well that improve the effectiveness of their communication:

- So what am I saying? First they ask rhetorical questions of themselves before their audience. They do this by saying *so what am I saying?* This allows them to add clarity in areas they know may be confusing;
- What I wanted to say! Second they will make purposeful mistakes or misstatements in order to point out and clarify what they said and what they meant. They do this by saying *That is not what I meant to say or this is the meaning in want to convey;*
- Said another way! Third they say it another way – They do this by saying *let me say that another way* so that rationalizers are alerted to listen to what is said – not for what they want to hear.

Chapter Five

An Uncommon Way of Seeing Ahead

"Where there is no vision, the people cast off restraint".
Proverbs 29:18

Remember the story of the stallion. What is it that keeps the heard together? It is the Stallion. The very existence of the heard and it what does and all it is able to accomplish is bound up in the existence of the Stallion. Without the stallion the heard would perish. The Stallion represents to the heard a vision. Within the concept of leadership, vision is a vivid and compelling description or view of how the future might unfold. Unlike the Stallion, vision is ultimately what keeps people together. Uncommon leaders have uncommon visions of future possibilities.

Stephen Covey, in his book "The 7 Habits of Highly Effective People" describes vision as habit number 2, "Beginning with the end in mind". By end he means that we should begin our days, our lives, and or our business with a clear image, picture, or paradigm of the end as our frame of reference for what we do today. He based "Begin with the end in mind" on the principle that all things are created twice. There is the mental or first creation and a physical or second creation to all things such as a blueprint comes before the house is built.

Uncommon leaders use vision to keep people self-focused on the destination when they would otherwise become distracted by their day to day tasks. Where there is no vision, the people cast off restraint. Said another way, the lack of vision is the main reason why people get off track and then often fail. Uncommon leaders

know this so they use vision to fight the natural tendencies of people to:
- Think and act in short term today segments only;
- Make vague plans for what will happen beyond today and;
- Live life or do business rather than build life and build business.

Vision is critical to challenging the unhealthy short term perspectives people develop. What is the time perspective of an alcoholic? It's the interval between drinks. What is time perspective of a sales person? It's the number of days before the next sale. The uncommon leader knows it is critical to solve the problems at hand but it is deadly to have no impact on the long term by what is done today.

Creating long term goals do not cause people to act with long term perspectives. The day to day drudgery of what has to be done today usually takes all the time people have to devote to today. Leaders use vision to change what drives others beneath the surface of life. The power of vision:
- Unites the hearts of people – they learn to think together, dream together and to act together;
- Gives life to purpose – people learn to fulfill a shared purpose;
- Intensifies the ability of people to see common ways;
- Helps people to see beyond where they saw before;
- Helps people to see faster than they saw before and;

- Helps people to see more than they saw before.

Covey says *we are more in need of a vision or destination and a compass (a set of principles or directions) and less in need of a road map.*

Understand that the way of the uncommon leader is to develop how others think and plan what they will do today. Vision is indispensible to keeping people aimed in the same direction and in keeping everyone on track.

Chapter Five — Lead More Manage Less

An Uncommon Way of Facilitating Control

"Most underperforming organizations usually are over managed and under led".
Warren Bennis

One of the things that differentiate uncommon leaders from others is learning to lead more and to manage less. I mentioned earlier that many people find it difficult to accurately distinguish between leading and managing. Though they are closely related leading and managing are profoundly different activities; one deal's with people and the other with the things people do. As Peter Drucker and Warren Bennis say *management is doing things right and leadership is doing the right things.*

The uncommon leader learns to use management as the tool to teach leaders to lead first and always and to manage as necessary. In my experience working with many businesses and leaders, I find that we have far too many people who are managers disguised as leaders. Remember our case study Watson. Watson was a bottom line guy. Management is too a bottom line focus; it asks how can I best accomplish the things I want. Leadership however is a top line focus. It asks what are the things we want to accomplish and why?

The path to effectiveness for the uncommon leader is littered with the uncommon ways they view the common things in life. Management is one of those things. Understanding that management is critical and complimentary to the success of the leader, the uncommon leader uses management in three ways that bring unique impact beyond the intent of management itself. Managers and management functions for the uncommon leader must always:

- Place why before what: Why this task or this function at this time and place helps the leader ensure that the right things done lead and things done right follows in support;
- Put principle before priority: In the natural order of things, leadership must come before management. It is a leadership principle that should never be circumvented by the seeming priority need to manage;
- Transform before conform: Things in the environment change rapidly today. Leaders must never permit the people or the businesses they lead to reach a peak. Management must be designed to allow natural transformation rather than natural conformation to a steady state.

In 2008, at my annual end of year Leadership Round Table, I discussed the leader's responsibility toward management with leaders from nine different organizations. Two things became clear to them at the end of our session. First, they had some difficulty themselves as did their people understanding the difference between when to lead and when to manage. Second, each of them could recount an instance where the organizations they led had worked on something the past year that wasn't a priority or didn't turn out to be the right thing to do. They realized leadership must come before management; that is the natural order of things.

Reverse them and you may find yourself setting records for growth but playing the wrong game.

Let me give you an example and contrast of leading and managing at work. The officials for my son's basketball games managed the games to ensure teams complied with all the rules of the game for fair play. The coaches were the leaders for each team; they were concerned with developing the overall game plan and then watching the games develop so that they could make the right decisions about plays to run or players to play. The game officials managed; and the coaches led. Here is a little table that illustrates the nature of leading and managing. It is not supposed to represent a complete listing rather to give you a sense of the difference between leading and managing:

Leading and Managing Contrast

Area	Leader	Manager
Essence	Development	Stability
Focus	Leading People	Managing work
Effectiveness	In the person	In authority
Appeal	To the heart	To the head
Style	Transformational	Transactional
Direction	New ways	Existing ways
Produces	Success	Output
Approach	Sets direction	Plans detail
Decisions	Facilitates	Makes

Chapter Five
Lead More Manage Less

Some of you are probably saying *I don't have time to search out new ways when I am struggling to make the existing ways work better.* For sure, seeming conflicts like this arise often. But the uncommon leader will always go back to asking is this the way I should be going in the first place.

My wife and I have survived raising four sons. We have raised them to be successful young adults. Along the way we were challenged beyond measure. We learned the hard way that we had to lead our children more than manage what we wanted them to do and to become.

We are friends with a couple who also have four children. With their second child, a daughter, they learned quickly they needed to be the leaders they had yet to become because managing her and what they wanted her to become was not going to work. Their daughter started driving when she was 16 years old. Before she turned 18 she was involved in three automobile accidents and she had four traffic tickets for moving violations. Fortunately her accidents were minor in terms of vehicle and property damage but sill the parents had to deal with the fallout. They attempted all the things any parent would do to manage the situation. They suspended her driving privileges; they restricted the times she was permitted to drive; they limited her to driving alone and so forth. Still they struggled through one accident after another.

Finally when they were at their wits end and they realized that their daughter just wasn't getting it they asked me for ideas. Their daughter was simply not a safe responsible driver and until that changed nothing they did was going to work. Being safe and responsible however starts with attitude more than skill. She had to want to become better – she had the skill to do it but she lacked the maturity and desire at that time.

I suggested to them that instead of managing her to failure they should try leading her to success. We sat down with their daughter one Sunday after church and said to her. *We are at our wits end with the way you take driving. You are a careless irresponsible driver and until that changes we cannot envision (that vision word) permitting you to ever be allowed to drive with your younger siblings or anyone else in the car with you. You are simply too unsafe.*

Together they calculated the number of miles she was absolutely required to drive each week – to school, work, church and some leisure. Then they told her each week she would be expected (not required nor restricted – but expected) to drive no more than the number of miles they calculated were absolutely required for her essential needs.

If she reached that number of miles driven before the end of the week the car would be shut down. She could even make an exception and permit herself to continue to drive until the next week rolled around but it would be her responsibility clear that with her parents and to act responsibly and to be personally accountable for how she led herself. The parents changed their role in all this from managing what she was doing to developing who she needed to become.

Finally they explained to her that they were going to do this because they could see a time in the near future where she would grow to be an exceptionally safe and responsible driver. They just needed to put her on that path and support her along the way. It's been 4 years since that time and she has not had an accident or traffic violation since. She is a much safer driver today than she was – safer at her age than the parents were was at her age. Their daughter told me later that she realized just how irresponsible she was and that by allowing her to figure it out that enabled her to see more than what her parents were trying to manage for her. Her parents had to learn to lead before they managed; to follow principle before priority and; to transform before they conformed.

Your life follows your attitude.

As the parents followed this approach they were still concerned about eliminating accidents and traffic violations. But they saw that the more emphasis they placed on managing the fallout from failure of the process the more the process was inclined to fail. They were trying to become efficient at navigating their way through the jungle but the leader in them climbed the tallest tree, surveyed the entire situation and yelled down to *we are in the wrong jungle!*

Let me offer a final word on leaders who incorporate a lead first then manage perspective in all their management functions. The greatest threat to developing a leadership environment where leaders are grown and then trained and equipped with the necessary management skills is one of attitude.

Much of this has to do with the attitudes we develop toward achieving results and the impatience we have with undeveloped people. The more we manage people the more people will try to manage themselves and or others; the more we control others the more control they will learn to exert. The more we lead people the more likely people will learn to start leading themselves more effectively. *A poorly motivated individual is a leadership issue; a poorly trained individual is a management issue. Motivation is more a function of attitude than training.* Yet we typically approach motivating an individual primarily with management tools rather than the strong but gentle arm of leadership.

The leader of one of the departments within the Secretary of the Army once told me *your life follows your attitude.* This leader was responsible for the development and performance of over 12 thousand people in support of over 500 thousand soldiers and Army civilians. Having a lead first attitude was critical to his people effectively serving the needs of US soldiers deployed across the world.

From Influence to Association

**"Jesus answered him, "What I am doing you do not understand now, but afterward you will understand".
John 13:7**

    A little later in the book I will speak to you about the need to influence others; but there is something even greater than influence uncommon leaders use to inspire people to achieve beyond what they thought they could do. I call it the law of association! It happens when people move beyond influence where they permit themselves to do things they may not have done otherwise, to association where they allow you inspire them to become people they did not dream they could become. There is no greater, no more effective or no more certain way to inspire, to motivate, to encourage or to influence others than the ability to achieve a state of association.

    Mastering the ability to do things in such a way that others get the full meaning and significance of your actions only after a period of time has passed is the best way to create association. The scripture above references a time when Jesus was washing His disciple's feet. When the disciples wondered why He would do that, He explained *what I do now you do not fully understand, but afterward you will understand.* Later after Jesus' death, the significance of Jesus' act of washing their feet came to them with the force of deep revelation and meaning. They realized, He wanted them to understand and to be willing to serve the needs of one another no matter their individual statuses or positions among people. Uncommon leaders do uncommon things with common things to bring about uncommon changes in the people they lead. If you learn nothing else from reading this book; if you decide to act on just one thing then let it be this. And you will transform your effectiveness and the effectiveness of many that know you. *Uncommon leaders learn that leadership is better caught than taught and doing great things that make no apparent sense initially is a great way to help others catch what you want them to learn.*

The law of association has the same inherent quality of goodness as leadership; this means it is an association that is inherently good for one and good for all. It is not association when it is meant to harm or when it is used for harmful destructive purposes. The law of association is the most uncommon and the most effective of all the ways the greatest of our uncommon leaders impact others. It is one of the most effective ways of connecting with others! Let me share several examples of how this law works.

In 1987, I was on military assignment to West Berlin Germany. If you recall, in 1987, the Berlin Wall was still standing as a reminder of the cold war. The Soviet Union and the Soviet Bloc countries – especially East Germany were still united. West Berlin was located 110 miles into what was then Communist East Germany. Berlin at the time it was a high stakes environment where you could look across the street and see the face of your enemy. I often wondered what kept things from blowing up. One nervous soldier on either side could have caused a global incident with catastrophic consequences. That was the environment for me and hundreds of other US service members, civilians and families at that time.

In June of 1987, then US President Ronald Reagan, visited West Berlin on the anniversary of the 250 year birthday of the city – a city divided – a city that at that time stood as a reminder and gateway of freedom for millions of eastern bloc soviet people who knew no freedom at all.

Arriving in Berlin on June 12, 1987, President and Ms. Reagan were taken to the Reichstag, where they viewed the Berlin Wall from a balcony. The wall itself encompassed West Berlin – it was just short of 100 miles around. I know because I ran the entire distance of the Wall several times while training to run the annual Berlin marathon. President Reagan then made his famous West Berlin speech at the Brandenburg Gate at 2:00P, in front of two panes of bulletproof glass protecting him from potential snipers.

Though we do not have official numbers or any way to confirm it, but we estimated there were over 200,000 East German citizens standing as close to the Wall as possible on their side listening to what the President said that day. They were not enemies; they wondered why we were not friends. About 45,000 people from West Berlin were in attendance; among them were West German President Richard Von Weizsacker, Chancellor Helmut Kohl and West Berlin Mayor Eberhard Diepgen. That afternoon Reagan said, *we welcome change and openness; for we believe that freedom and security go together, that the advance of human liberty can only strengthen the cause of world peace. There is one sign the Soviets can make that would be unmistakable, that would advance dramatically the cause of freedom and peace. General Secretary Gorbachev, if you seek peace, if you seek prosperity for the Soviet Union and Eastern Europe; if you seek liberalization; come here to this gate. Mr Gorbachev, open this gate. Mr Gorbachev, Mr Gorbachev, tear down this wall!*

History cannot be certain what if any impact President Reagan's speech had on the crumbling of the wall a mere two years later. But history does record that there was a great division within the Reagan camp on whether or not it was advisable for him to challenge Mr Gorbachev to tear down the wall. In the end, after much debate in the Reagan camp, it is recorded that Reagan himself said to his supporters *we'll keep it in.*

I bet the estimated 200,000 East Germans who heard the speech where were happy that he did. You see, we had 200,00 people that day on the East German side of the wall who came to associate with President Reagan because he represented the opposite of what the Wall had come to mean in their lives. What President Reagan did then we did not nor could anyone in East Germany or the Soviet Union understand, but they soon did. We could be friends.

But even before 1987, back in 1985, President Reagan had demonstrated the far reaching and profound positive impact we could have doing what others do not understand. It was during the Geneva Summit with the Soviet leader in November 1985. History records that at one moment during the summit, President Reagan said to Mr Gorbachev *You know, people have come to think of us as enemies. But we don't have to be what they say!*

Now we don't know if this thought planted in 1985 and less than two years later the invitation to tear down the wall impacted Gorbachev. But again history records that after the Soviet Bloc fall Reagan and Gorbachev became as close to friends as two people could be described for what were seemingly two bitter enemies.

Take a look at the illustration next. It will help you understand how the law of association takes influence to an even higher level:

The Law of Association

Areas of Connection	Influence	Law of Association
Identification	What they do	Who they become
Impact	People learn from you	People learn of you
How people are touched	Minds are impacted	Lives are transformed
How people are recognized	Identification is by you	Identification is in you
Core	Gives meaning to purpose	Gives purpose to life

Over the past 10 years, I have worked with many businesses, privately and publically held; governments at all levels from local jurisdictions to nations; and non-profit organizations in many areas.

Chapter Six

I have conducted leadership seminars that have touched hundreds of people. I have found few if any business, organization, team or individual know of and or understand the power of the law of association as it relates to developing people of uncommon effectiveness. The few who do get it have several things in common I want to share with you here:

- They are uncommonly transparent;
- Their humility is their greatest strength and;
- Caring is their greatest leadership virtue.

Transparency – The Greatest Source of Trust

Why are uncommon leaders uncommonly transparent? Transparency helps keep the leader accountable and it helps others learn transparency is critical to being successful leaders. Diane Ravitch, a Research Professor of Education at New Your University and a historian of education uses the quote *the person who knows how will always have a place in life. The person who knows why will inevitably be the leader.* Uncommon leaders achieve their transparency from their comfort in sharing with others the why of things. They know the mind is very inquisitive and people often need to understand why things are done in order to close the gap in their own thinking. The uncommon leader knows that people will either reason or rationalize their way through life. Those who reason will ask what and the look at everything to determine if things can be understood; those who rationalize will say this is what they want to know and then they will sort through things to find what they need to support what they believe.

The uncommon leader knows we need more people to reason than to rationalize so they gladly share why as a function of explaining what. Sharing why also reveals the motives of the leader. Revealing their motives is a way to keep leaders honest with themselves and with others. Shelia Murray, author, says *Many organizations and individuals have gone completely off course because they first asked how to do something instead of first asking why they should do it.* Jim Collins of "Good to Great" speaks of asking why about a position several times in order to get to the fundamental reason for what a business wants to do.

Asking why enables you, your business, your organizations to get in touch with the fundamental reason you do what you do; you are able to start on track and stay on track because you question your motives for what you want to do as a precondition for sharing with others what you'd like to do. Look at it this way.

Leading with the Transparency of Explaining Why

Leading with Why	Which makes	What is to be done
Starts and keeps you on an honest track	⟶	Unquestionably appropriate for the circumstance
Serves to reinforce what is preeminent	⟶	The most important priority
Invites focus on the purity of motives	⟶	A greater reason to do things well
Starts you from the right place	⟶	Keep busy staying on the right path
Reveals the reason why things will work	⟶	Inspires determination to make things work

The leader of uncommon effectiveness speaks in a why fashion. They do not wait to be asked why; they speak to others in terms of why before getting to what. This method of communication with others reveals the leader's values, principles and their truest motives and desires. There is nothing to hide or hidden that they are not willing to share. They have a child-like openness and comfort in exposing what gives them the ideas they have.

This transparency makes them uncommonly effective before others. When people can see clearly the heart of a leader they are more likely to move past being influenced to reaching a level of association with the leader. When people associate with their leader they work beyond their potential to be successful first for the organization, then for the leader and finally for themselves. People learn to reflect the same great virtues the leader is known for.

Here is one more example of the power of sharing why and the impact it has on businesses and individuals. I recently conducted a strategic planning session for a mid-sized privately held company. In many years of conducting planning sessions I have learned that most leaders come to the sessions with the goals they desire already in their minds. So as each session starts, I always ask the leaders of the organization to share with me the goals they already have in their minds.

Typically I will get seven to ten goals which I capture on a white board so that we can return to them later at the appropriate point during the session. Then when we arrive at the point during the session to identify the planning goals, I challenge the teams to ask why a goal important to their clients? Why is it important to your customer that you increase revenue? The response might be to sustain growth. Why is it important to sustain growth? The response might be to reward shareholders. Why is it important to reward shareholders? The response might be they keep us in business. Why is it important to stay in business? The response at this point might be because we exist to serve the needs of our customers.

I might then ask why then do we not have a goal that says improve the quality of service we provide to our customers? Do you see the point? Asking why can get you to the true meaning and purpose and reason for all your desires.

Chapter Six
The Source of Trust

The uncommon leader speaks straight forward in this way – always speaking from the core of things so that others know instinctively why the business, why the family, why the team is going to do what it does; they understand and have the courage to lead by stating why because it's the foundation for making the appropriate things happen at the appropriate times. They know why being accountable is important to creditability and trust; why openness and truthfulness are the surest ways to build relationships of the highest integrity; why values are important to anchoring the business and its people to a strong unshakable foundation and why humility builds strong authentic relationships and it kills the presence of the ego or arrogance.

Chapter Six

Humility – The Greatest Source of Strength!

I shared with you earlier that I love to play a round of golf. It is such a challenging sport and one where you compete with yourself to overcome your shortcomings. Golf is a sport of paradox. In order to hit the ball far you must learn to grip the club lightly and swing the club smoothly. When your instincts say to hit it far you must grip it and rip it, the natural laws of the game say the opposite. It makes no sense at the beginning but any serious golfer learns this lesson later on. You might hear your golf coach say *it may not make sense to you now but it will as you learn golf fundamentals.*

The uncommon leader knows the lesson of the paradox when it comes to their core attitude or disposition. They are not humble leaders because they want to be strong; they are strong people with a stronger sense of humility. Others are drawn to them because in their humility they focus all their strength on what is best for others. They have a you first and not be first attitude; they have such a sense of gratitude for the privilege of leading others that they are driven beyond what is common to transform, elevate and achieve significance with others and with their business. This paradoxical sense of humble strength is the thing that draws others to them; it is what gives them their strength to do more; to achieve more; and to be more for others.

Humility does not mean false modesty; it is not the pretense of taking a back seat in order to make a point. Humility is the genuine feeling and presence of child-like transparency; it is making others feel the importance of their lives as the same or greater than anyone else; it means the freedom of not having to think about yourself at all.

The poet T.S. Eliot says *Humility is the most difficult of all virtues to achieve; nothing dies harder than the desire to think well of self.* Nothing lives greater in the uncommon leader than the desire to think well and do well for others. It is in that paradox of living they achieve uncommon strength. You may not understand now what great source of strength is found in humility, but walk the path of humility and you will understand. People more easily associate with the humble; humility is a virtue desired by many but achieved by only a few.

Caring – The Greatest Leadership Virtue!

Remember leadership has an inherent quality of goodness. People who lead to unjust ends or using unjust means are not leaders but misleaders because their leadership lacks the critical quality of virtue. Virtue is the quality of being morally excellent and it is valued as a foundation of principle and goodness. If in humility others know that I have their interests at heart; by virtue they feel the goodness of those interests shed forth into their lives. In simple terms, caring is virtue and goodness of leadership being given by the leaders to others.

I provide businesses and individual the service of what I call a Structured Interview Assessment. The structured interview is designed to help leaders understand "what makes a great person great". The process is a 45 minute individual dialogue designed to determine the degree to which an individual demonstrates a set of competencies believed to be crucial to their success in the role they are assigned.

Our findings in this objective assessment typically correlate with what business leaders see in the daily performance of each individual. But perhaps the most important finding for us is not determining what we expect but it is to stumble into what we do not expect.

When we look at the data collected from assessing over 150 leaders in 2009, we find an uncommon development. About 10 percent of the individuals assessed demonstrated a quality and aspect of person we did not anticipate; they demonstrated a sense of genuine caring for others, for the customers, for the clients and for everyone. When we shared this insight with leaders of the businesses we found we had discovered the key competence that made uncommon people more effective than others. We did not set out to determine if caring was a competence critical to leader success but we found caring had a greater impact on success than any other singular competence.

> *Dad once looked down at an assembly line of women and thought, "These are all like my own mom – they have kids, homes to take care of, people who need them." It motivated him to work hard to give them a better life because he saw his mom in all of them. That's how it all begins – with fundamental respect and empathy – he cared.*
>
> **Bob Galvin, CEO**
> **Speaking of his father, founder of Motorola**

I have assessed over 300 high level individuals for companies all over. I have modified the process to focus more directly on the degree to which an individual understands why caring matters and the degree to which they demonstrate caring as a personal and professional virtue. Typically I will make the statement *people who work for you say you care about them, convince me that you do.*

Unfortunately more than a few people sometimes respond with comments such as *I keep personal and professional things separate;* or *people don't have to like me they just have to do what I need them to do;* or *I am who I am and people who work for me have to learn that.*

These are people who miss the whole point of leading. They not only miss out on understanding why caring is important, they do not understand what works or how it works. Those who do understand tell me the things they do for others – things like giving them time off; working schedules around to accommodate emergencies; giving them greater responsibilities and so forth. These are the people who keep a fairly good sense of harmony in the work environment for others. They care because they need to not because it is who they are.

But then there is the uncommon leader who understands why caring is crucial to how others eventually perform. They responded with comments like *I get to know them and I let them know who I am; I spend time with others and I allow them to spend time with me; and finally a few will even say I tell them verbally and I support that by my actions.* People may not need to like you as a leader but they certainly must not dislike you and they cannot be effective being indifferent toward you or by simply tolerating you as a person and as the leader.

The U.S. Army has eleven leadership principles by which each leader is expected to lead others; one of those principles is to know your soldiers and to care for their welfare. The Army understands the leader who does not demonstrate a sense of caring is not a leader at all but simply the person in charge today.

I am reminded of a story told about Nazi Germany and the end of World War II. A German Sergeant informed the members of his platoon that they would probably soon be assigned to go fight the Russians near the Russian front lines. A soldier in the platoon who had only just been called to the Army in the last year was the only person who responded to the Sergeant. The soldier said he would not go fight along the Russian front for the Nazi Army because he did not believe in what they stood for; he said he did not believe the Army cared about Germans because they did not seem to care about others (reference to the Jews of course).

The Sergeant asked the soldier how it was that someone who had only been in the Army less than a year could know that the Nazi leadership and the German Army did not care about the German people. *We are at war because we care* shouted the Sergeant! The young soldier responded by explaining to the Sergeant and others in the platoon that Nazi leaders and the Army did understand the future impact their actions would have on the conscious of the German people. He explained that the Nazi leadership and the Army could not possibly care about the German people because they killed so many innocent people who had nothing to do with the war and that in the end, the German people would be left to live with the deaths of so many on their conscious.

The comment caused the whole platoon to speak up in opposition to the orders they expected. The story had a sad ending because it's said the Sergeant promptly shot and killed the young German soldier in order to put down the small rebellion that was about to flare up. In the end the young soldier was another death that would live on the conscious of the German people.

People will not form an associative relationship with those they do not care about or with those whom they believe do not care for them. They may work for an uncaring leader but not with their hearts. They will not perform to their highest potential but only to the minimal standards to keep the leader off their backs.

Former General and Chief of Staff of the US Army Eric Shinseki said, *to be an effective leader you must love those you lead. You can command without that sense of commitment but you cannot lead without it. And without leadership, command is a hollow experience often filled with mistrust and arrogance.* When we are not caring and empathetic leaders others stop being authentic; they stop bringing talent and energy into the work place and they stop bringing feelings into the pursuit and performance of the goals we set for them (Cooper & Sawaf,).

Developing an Effective Leadership Style

"To lead people, walk beside them. The best leaders, the people do not notice their existence. The next best, the people will honor and praise. The next best, the people will fear. And the next best, the people will hate. When the best leader's work is done the people say we did it ourselves"!
Lao-tsu

What is style?

We often struggle with understanding style? What is leadership style? Is it the flare and charisma of Mother Teresa, Winston Churchill or a Bill Clinton? Is it the strength and command presence of a Colin Powell? Or is it the inspirational traits of Walt Disney or Martin Luther King Jr.? Many historians consider Adolph Hitler to have been a charismatic leader like Mother Teresa and Winston Churchill and Bill Clinton. But Hitler was very different from these leaders. So then how do we explain the difference between them?

So what are we missing? What is it that gives one person uncommon interpersonal effectiveness? It may be more appropriate to say Hitler used a dictatorial or autocratic approach for the situation tempered with a charismatic manner of engaging with people. Mother Teresa used a collaborative approach for the situations she faced and humble servant manner with the people she engaged. We make this contrast to highlight a nuance of leadership style.

Style is really the combination of the approach or tool the leader chooses to use for the situation and the manner by which the leader uses the tool with people. In some instances, such as with Mother Teresa, the tool and the manner it's used are or could be very similar or even the same. But in the case with Hitler, he used an autocratic governing process for the situation and his charm and charisma with people especially those outside Germany.

Problems with leadership style occur when we do not choose the appropriate approach and tool for the situation or when we use an ineffective relational manner with people. Remember Watson. At the outset of our relationship, Watson's personal approach with situations and his manner with people were the same. He was a very strong directive person. Remember his idea of a leader was the first one to be first. He just wanted the kids to win! Watson believed that results mattered most and in the end getting the results he desired was the evidence of his effectiveness as a leader. So he used a directive approach for the situations and a directive approach with people.

He learned later as he worked through our leadership program that his overall style was very ineffective. People had difficulty focusing on the results he achieved because the manner in which he approached people was so dramatically offensive. Watson's directive style of leadership stood out in a negative way more than the results he achieved.

So then there are two components of leadership style which you must master in order to achieve the effectiveness you have within your potential. These are to know the most appropriate approach to take for the situation you face and then knowing which relational manner is going to be most effective to engage people within that situation.

You can learn fairly easily the approach to take for the situation at hand. For example a situation where consensus of thought and action is needed would likely require a participative approach while an emergency situation that demands quick action might require a directive approach. You get the idea? In most instances the situation is going to dictate for you the approach you should take to achieve success. Pay attention to the situation and you will less likely choose an ineffective leadership approach.

Knowing and choosing the most effective relational manner for the people within a situation may be a little more difficult to learn. I like to think of your relational manner with people as the flavor that gives your approach to situations its distinctive quality of goodness. It is like adding salt in the right amount to the food you eat. Just as the appropriate use of salt brings out the hidden quality of the great taste in what we eat, so is the choice and use of our relational manner with others important to how we bring out our best for the people we lead. Too much salt and you not only ruin the taste of the food

The manner you choose to relate with people can either bring out the best in others or it can kill the best in others.

but you ruin the food as well. It's a choice we can make!

Uncommon leaders develop a seeming inherent nature to clearly see these two aspects of style and to act in such a natural way to blend and balance them in achieving uncommon success with the situations through a highly effective interpersonal manner with people. You can learn to develop your style and to blend the components of style just as effectively as the great leaders do it. Just remember the approach must be appropriate for the situation – that may change as the situation dictates. But the flavor of your approach, the manner you engage people, is probably going to be more consistent – it is the quality of you that enables you to engage effectively with people no matter the situation.

But before we go further into determining what style is right for you let's discuss leadership style in a little more detail. I could write a book just on style alone; most young and developing leaders – those who are just learning about leadership, are most intrigued to learn about the different styles of leadership. In our development program, I must often work to change what people think about leadership style because they have not had good examples from which to learn.

Many people think of style as something they try on to see if it fits them; your style should be something you do in a way that is useful for others. It is not about what feels good to you but what is good for others. If you find and or use a leadership style that is a great fit for you – then you will probably run the risk of wearing it to the wrong occasions and trying to effectively engage the wrong people with it. Watson and others you probably know stand out in negative ways because their approach does not seem to fit the occasion or the styles they used was not right for people.

One size does not fit all people or all circumstances. Uncommon leaders adapt to others more than they try to change others; they adapt to the circumstance as the most effective way to change a circumstance. During our executive development programs, participants are often surprised to learn they must become effective using several styles of leadership when improving their current style was perhaps the reason they were attending our program.

Uncommon leaders don't know any more than you or I do now about the most effective leadership styles. Where they are different is in how they use a disciplined process and follow a path that leads to effectiveness. They examine each situation to determine what style is most appropriate and then they have the courage to use that style. They are not wedded to any one particular way of approaching the situations they face daily.

This is how they are different from you today. What makes the uncommon leader seem greater and more effective than others is the natural way they seem to balance or blend the right style with the right interpersonal flavor. Why are they able to do this? I believe it is because they have developed a greater than normal sense of self-awareness.

You remember self-awareness. It is one of Goleman's five components of Emotional Intelligence and it is within the personal dimension of our three dimensions of leadership. Self-awareness is important to building strong positive relationships not just in business, but in your homes, in your marriages, with your children and with your peers.

The more aware you are about who you are the more likely you will be willing to make the changes in yourself that are needed to harness stronger interpersonal relationships. So how well do you know yourself? A fundamental aspect of understanding your natural style is to understand yourself. Most young developing or immature leaders think about or spend lots of time trying to improve the performance or behaviors of others. In contrast, during my work with uncommon leaders and other leaders in our development programs I find that they spend over 60% of their time working to overcome challenges to improving their own effectiveness. Changing themselves, especially their behaviors, is the quickest way to changing others.

There are five challenges common to us all that we must consistently work to overcome if we are to become and remain effective leaders. These are:
- Self-leadership – learning to be effective with the self and learning to overcome or to limit the negative impact your leadership has on others;
- Positional leadership – learning that the position you hold is actually a limiting factor in developing effective leadership so you must learn to use positional leadership sparingly;

- Goals-driven leadership – learning that goals-focused leadership actually lead to creating busy-work for many people rather than work that is of value to the person and the organization;
- Apathy and indifference toward leadership – uncommon leaders work very diligently to never grow tired from the challenge to lead and finally;
- Transactional leadership – overcoming the constant desire we have as people and business to complete more tasks as the basis of our successes.

The first of these challenges is improving the way you lead yourself – your self- leadership. It shouldn't surprise you to find that sometimes it is your leadership that is the problem with the performance of others; people are not always the issue. *I have seen countless leaders in important roles become frustrated to the point of failing because they spend most of their time trying to understand the makeup of the people they lead when they do not understand first why they lead themselves the way they do.*

Individual Assessment

In our development program we have all leaders participate in an objective self-assessment as a basis for determining what areas they need to change most. It helps people to really understand who they are at their natural state.– if there is such a thing. Each leader who takes our program is invited to take an online objective assessment called the PDP® ProScan. Here is a short overview of the PDP.

PDP® ProScan is a quick, easy and reliable survey tool that is one of the most advanced instruments available. Statistical research of working adults enables the powerful ProScan Survey to produce reliable results to accurately assess a person's basic and preferred work and leadership styles. In less than 10 minutes, individuals mark to what degree they believe 60 different descriptors match their characteristics and how they believe others perceive them.

The survey examines combinations of specific traits that affect how the person works most effectively and reacts under stress. ProScan focuses on strengths and motivators to help people create an environment that reduces stress while improving energy and morale.

PDP® measures four cornerstone behavioral traits – Dominance, Extroversion, Pace (Patience) and Conformity. These traits influence leadership style. All traits can lead but each will do it with the unique style associated with that trait.

ProScan reports measure:

- How a person functions most naturally
- The role a person feels they need to play
- How a person predictably comes across to others
- Energy resources
- Satisfaction index
- Stress levels
- Energy drain
- Decision-making style
- Leadership Style
- Communication Style
- Motivators
- De-motivators

There are a multitude of facets that make PDP unique.

- Creating a people management system designed for and used by organizations—its executives, owners, managers, and leaders
- Researching the working, adult population—for they are the next Top Performer within your organization, and
- Delivering results quickly, reliably and as accurately as possible

PDP's Integrated Management System is a proven program, making the business of people management more effective, scientific, and predictable. The core of PDP is the ProScan Survey and its resulting comprehensive reporting. The data is then analyzed by PDP's proprietary online application, generating complete, easily-interpreted reports for individuals and executives. From there, the PDP Management System, including JobScan and TeamScan, is applied and implemented.

Then during the first two hours of our development program we have an expert from the PDP come in and explain the results of the assessment to the participants. We do this because it is helpful for each person to have a better understanding of who they are as people before we dive too deeply into who we want them to become as leaders.

Remember our analogy of m*onkeys do what monkey do*. The focus of our leadership development program is to help put each person on a path to transforming themselves from one thing to another. To do this well each person should know instinctively who they are at prior to starting any development program.

You can learn more about the PDP in the chapter on PDP. We have included a special invitation to allow you to take the PDP assessment if you are interested in learning some things about yourself that you didn't know before.

Common Leadership Styles

In the book "Primal Leadership," Daniel Goleman and his Emotional Intelligence work describes six different styles of leadership. The most effective leaders can move among these styles adopting the one that meets the situation at the moment. Each style becomes part of the leader's toolkit for becoming effective.

- The Visionary Style – This style is most appropriate when people and or the organization lack direction. Goleman contends the visionary leader articulates where people and or the business needs to go but not necessarily how they are to get there;

- The Coaching Style – This style is most appropriate when you want to develop others and to improve their performance. It is the style I have chosen to use in writing this book. Coaching works when there is a discernable need to close the gaps in the performance of people today and where they need to be tomorrow. It is all about enabling people and or businesses reach the full potential of their capabilities;

- The Affiliative Style – This style emphasizes the importance of team work and focuses on creating harmony in teams by connecting people to each other. Goleman says this style is appropriate when there is a need to heighten team harmony, increase support of one another and improve communication in an organization;

- The Democratic Style – This style is appropriate when the leader must tap into the collective wisdom of the organization to pursue an objective or when the way forward is unclear or undecided;
- The Pacesetting Style – This style is appropriate where goals and objectives are set and the leader needs to set the pace and focus for others to stay on task;
- The Commanding Style – This style suggests classic military type leadership, is appropriate when the situation requires quick action of a very directive nature where a well- trained and effective response is required.

Goleman is not the author of all styles of leadership. Others such as the supportive, directive or delegative are just a few. The point to remember about your style of leadership is this. You must adapt your style to the situation at hand; the leader must be more adaptive than the led. Using a style that is inappropriate for the situation is like trying to put out a small fire using gasoline because gasoline is wet. You won't get the results you desire unless you use the right tools.

Remember our discussion of skills and competencies. Knowing which style to use for a situation is a learned skill. It identifies you among those who can't. But competence is the manner by which you use the style within the situation. It is what separates you from among those who can; and this is what makes the uncommon leader uncommon. The uncommon leader takes the time to sharpen the axe before starting the work to chop the tree while the good leader takes any axe available without regard to whether the axe is sharp.

Style - Critical Characteristics

In 2008 and 2009, we used the executives who took development programs to survey feedback around the question of what they believed made them good leaders. We asked a hundred executives *what characteristic or quality of their style was most responsible for giving it a distinguishable mark of high quality and excellence?* We gave each person five options from which to choose but we allowed them to add an option for "other" if one of the five wasn't right for them. The options we gave them were the characteristics and or traits people in our programs most often offer as reasons for their effectiveness. They were: competence, integrity, dedication, fairness and decisiveness. Here is how they responded:

Distinguishing Leadership Styles

Characteristic / Quality	Number of Responses
Competence	13
Integrity	14
Dedication	12
Fairness	41
Decisiveness	12
Other	7

Here is what I found when I closely examined their responses. While competence, integrity, dedication, fairness and decisiveness are important competencies they did not give leadership style its distinctive mark of excellence. The default we have as people is to expect our leaders to be competent; we expect them to be people of integrity; we expect them to be dedicated because they have that expectation of us; we want them to know when they are fair and unfair and; we would like them to be decisive because we know decisiveness is critical to moving forward at a good pace. All these things we expect of our leaders anyway. So they are not the best indicators of what gives style its excellence. Each attribute was more important to making the individual style of leadership more complete than elite.

When we asked a group of uncommon leaders who attended our year end Executive Round Table discussions the same question we got a vastly different and more insightful response. We did not to give them the five options we gave the other group. Rather we simply asked the uncommon leaders to consider the question and to offer their responses. This is what we found. Uncommon leaders view the same things from very different perspectives. The uncommon leaders, there were only 10 of them, had only three responses between them. Four of them said respect for others was most important; four said people focus was their most important; and two said character / integrity was most important.

In examining their responses more closely and in comparing them to the group of high potential leaders we discovered an underlying principle. Leaders from our first group, our good leaders, viewed their styles as containing their distinctive traits of effectiveness; they believed when their approach to the situation was right this made their approach with people right as well.

But the uncommon leaders viewed their traits as separate from but key ingredients to making their styles distinctively excellent. Style is insufficient unless the uncommon leader gives it something to bring out its life. So they use three traits, respect for others, people focus and character / integrity to clearly put the emphasis on others more than the situation or the self. In other words they add to their overall style an effective manner with people to make their approach more effective for the situations. This way through their overall style they connect with others with more heart and will than with competence and skill. So just what is important about respect for others, people focus and character / integrity?

Style – Respect for Others / People Focus

I believe the characteristics of respect for others and people focus can be found in the empathy component of Daniel Goleman's Emotional Intelligence of leaders. Empathy is the ability to be fully acquainted with the emotional state of others and the skill to treat people according to their emotional needs. Empathy gives the leader an intuitive sense of knowing what people feel and the humility to acknowledge this awareness in words and deeds. Empathy acknowledges the other person's competence and value thereby creating an atmosphere of reciprocal giving.

When people believe they give more to a relationship than what they get in return, they feel distressed and typically either reduce inputs (coming to work late or missing meetings, gossiping, careless work), or they increase complaints (ask for transfers or better working conditions or in the end they may even end the relationship). And though the word empathy might sound non-businesslike and out of place with the tough realities of running an effective business, it is perhaps the most powerful contributor to the success of people in business today. Empathy simply means the leader thoughtfully considers the feelings of others along with any other business or organizational factors in the path to making intelligent decisions. People respond well to those whom they believe understand and consider their feelings.

The uncommon leader's use of empathy in illuminating their leadership style is a powerful and effective tool to help them to say the right things in the right ways and at the right times. Without empathy the leader would likely be perceived to be uncaring or detached. Take a look at the table below:

The Empathic and Detached Leader

Leader	With Empathy	Without Empathy
Core relational skill	Leaders project a caring respectful attitude	Leaders risk projecting a detached, uncaring, selfish and conceited attitude
Insight into others	Leaders see the whole picture and can envision how others will be affected	Leaders overlook the human aspect of decisions, impacts and thus miss out on possible impacts on others
Collaborative effectiveness	The leader shares thoughts and ideas which leads to greater acceptance of different perspectives	The leader makes individual judgments without the benefit of the thoughts of others; others are unwilling to share true feelings. Leaders don't listen well and they often miss clues about the true feelings of others.
Leader resonance	Leaders connect with a greater portion of those they engage; trust is born	Leaders disengage with many they attempt to connect with ; trust is rarely evidenced toward the leader

Style - Character and Integrity!

Where then does character and integrity fit with our styles? If the empathy to focus on and to respect others is the flavor of your leadership style, character and integrity are the high lights of your style; they are the factors that illuminate. Character and integrity give your style an uncommon sense of being of the highest quality. Work that is the highest quality cannot easily be mistaken. Professional people who do high quality work are different from people who want to do good work. The foundation then for quality and excellence is found in leaders whose leadership style is illuminated by uncompromising character and integrity.

These leaders are driven to be right and to always develop themselves to be the *best* at something. They learn to reject their own marginal efforts and to be driven to always deliver more than is expected. Flaws in their character and or flaws in their integrity will manifest itself in the quality of their leadership and in their work.

So what are we saying? Uncommon leaders use their character and integrity to illuminate the inherent quality of their leadership style; it is consistently professional always. They use empathy or respect for others / people focus – choose your words – as a way to add the distinctive flavor to their style. Because of this they usually speak and act in ways so that their words and actions are graceful, seasoned with respect and with empathy toward others. By leading in this way others are generally more willing to accept even a difficult message with uncommon responsibility and understanding. They respond better.

Here is what I have learned about great leadership style. It is the bottom line, as Watson would say, for leaders who want a more effective style than what they have today.

Effectiveness of Leadership Style

Style	Objective	Action	Outcome
Inspirational	Gain buy-in	Explain why before what	Buy in – People commit to you before they buy into your plan
Supportive	Recover from mistakes	Focus forward on the things that are working	Positive attitudes – People solve problems faster and more effectively
Visionary	Set direction and course	Explain the plan – define roles not goals	Dependability – Creates better teamwork and a sense of personal accountability
Participative	Improve quality	Plant seeds of excellence – inspect what is expected	Greatness – Creates people who internalize quality efforts needed for quality outcomes
Coaching	Overcome performance challenges	Use tasks to develop talent in people	Competence – Builds stronger individual and organizational capability
Charismatic	Improve communication	Spend time with others	Trust – Creates people and an organization that are flexible and adaptable to change

Chapter Seven

Choose a leadership approach that is right for the situation but develop the interpersonal manner of engaging others that is best for people. Do this and you will put yourself on the path to achieving uncommon leadership effectiveness with your style.

| Footprints | Chapter Eight | The Leader We Want |

An Uncommon Leader's Job Announcement

"If you look to lead, invest 40% of your time leading yourself – your ethics, character,; principles, purpose, motivation and conduct. Invest at least 30% of your time leading those with authority over you and 15% leading your peers. Use the remainder to induce those you "work for" to understand and practice these principles. I use the term "work for" advisedly, for if you don't understand that you should be working for your mislabeled "subordinates", you haven't understood anything".
Dee Hock, CEO
Visa International

This is a very insightful and powerful quote from one man about what it takes to be a leader. What do we understand about what it really means to be a leader? Remember Watson the basketball parent. After a period of self-evaluation, Watson realized how difficult it would be for him to follow his own leadership. He reasoned that another Watson simply wouldn't like the way the first Watson led. We ask this question during our development programs. Would I Follow Me? My experience is that greater than 90% of the leaders in our programs initially respond yes to this question. After some discussion about what it really means to lead and what is really required to follow, that number might drop to 50%. Still I believe a 50% "yes" rate is probably higher than it should be. I believe the percentage should be no greater than 15%. Here is why.

If you desire the role of leader, you desire a role of incomparable importance with anything else. No role can compare to the importance of and the impact the leader will have on the life,

Chapter Eight — The Leader We Want

growth and development of individuals and on families; on the prosperity and value of businesses and on the development and opportunities nations can afford and provide for people. Desiring to be a leader should not be taken lightly.

My first assignment as a Second Lieutenant in the Army is where I learned how important it is to be a leader. On my first day I spit shinned my boots, starched my fatigues and reported in to my boss, an Army Major. He greeted me warmly and then pointed to a small table in the corner of his office and said *there is your desk.* I looked at him and said *but I was told my office was across the hall from you.* He told me the office across the hall was reserved for the Assistant Human Resources Officer and since I had asked to take the position of a leader in the organization the best space he had for me would be in the corner in his office.

Well I promptly corrected him. I had asked for the position of Assistant HR officer; I didn't recall asking for a position of leader. He told me when I volunteered to wear the uniform and when I accepted a commission as an officer in the Army, I was asking to be a leader; this is the way it is with many people and many roles. People look for positions to match their talent for what they do well while the reality is most roles need people to be someone talent can't make you.

So for the first three months of my assignment in that unit I sat in the corner of my boss' office. I watched and observed how he operated as a leader. He never asked me to excuse myself even when he was being challenged by his boss who was an Army

Chapter Eight — The Leader We Want

Colonel. At the end of 90 days, my boss told me if I still wanted to be a leader I could take the office across the hall and if I didn't think I wanted to be a leader I could take the office anyway. His job description, he told me, was to make me a leader and others like me.

After that assignment and for the remainder of my 20 plus year Army career, I had almost the same experience daily as I worked for very senior military leaders up to a Four Star General and for senior Department of Defense civilian leaders and very senior political leaders appointed by the President of the United States.

After retiring from the military I have continued my development as a leader by having the opportunity to work with leaders of uncommon effectiveness from business to education; and from state and local governments to church leadership all over the United States and internationally.

Through our development programs we have developed what we believe to be the perfect leader job announcement. Here you will find the uncommon ways leaders of uncommon effectiveness think and act to become uncommon people for the people and the organizations in which they belong. Our job announcement is posted by an organization, a family, a marriage, a small business, a government office and many other entities that have suffered through common leadership. They have come to realize that uncommon leadership is needed to enable them to achieve more of what their potential will allow them to achieve.

Chapter Eight

Job Announcement

Position Title: Uncommon Leader – All our positions require leaders. We have no non leaders in any organization of ours. Everyone is either a leader or working towards becoming a leader. We have found the organization works best when each person views themselves in this way. Generally we have found leaders more than non-leaders have learned to work best with others so it is a real plus for us to develop leaders all around and at all levels of the organization. Please do not worry if you believe your specific job function does not clearly require you to lead. We are certain that as a leader your job functions will be easier to accomplish when you see yourself as a leader.

Company Name: We have no particular company in mind for you at the moment. The reality is that once you become the leader, we think you can name any place that you touch and operate and there you will find the need to lead.

Company Industry: We have requirements for leaders in every company, every business, every home and family, every marriage and in every aspect of the social and private sectors. In fact our roles are everywhere and in everything because they are vitally important to the livelihood of people.

Job Function: Leadership – we describe leadership as individual effectiveness and success at achieving results by influencing and developing the self; by influencing and developing others and by enabling others to do the same. As you can see from our description, this role will require you to work on yourself a lot in order to develop the competence to work with others. As our leaders learn patience; they develop other leaders to be patient. As our leaders learn to be professionals in all things they develop other leaders to be professionals in all things as well. In this way you and others are able to be successful beyond your job roles in the businesses in which you will operate.

We know this type of job function is different from what you may have experienced in the past where the leader is expected to get things done with people. Our leadership role is different in that our guiding principle is to develop leaders who develop leaders who accomplish great things. We hope you will find this view interesting and exciting; and if you do not, don't worry about that. It is the expectation of our leaders to help transform how you think about the role you will play for us so that in a short time we are certain you will share our perspectives about leading and what it means to others and to the businesses in which we operate.

Entry Level: Any Level. We have leader roles at any and all levels in the company. We realize people are at different places experientially and developmentally but leader is a status every person can achieve and wear well. Since we want people demonstrating great leadership competency at where ever they are in our organizations and businesses we always start your development as a leader at the place you are today.

Employment Type: Full-time doesn't adequately describe the way we see your time as a leader. Lifetime is perhaps a better description of how we view it. We develop you to be a leader not for our organization but for the organizations we serve. So for example, our customers deserve that we engage with them through the effectiveness of uncommon leaders not followers; our vendors require the exceptional expertise of uncommon leaders and; our partners require much the same.

As we have grown to produce leaders the way we do, even the homes and families of the our leaders have the expectation that we will send home to them each day a more effective leader than what came to us at the start of the day. So for us the type of employment we offer is for you to offer your life for whatever time that remains to be a leader of uncommon effectiveness.

Salary Requirements: Before we discuss the specific job requirements of the role of our leaders we want to address your salary requirements. We understand salary requirements are usually negotiated later in the employment process but we have learned that when we have this discussion now it will be to your greater overall personal and professional satisfaction and benefit later.

You see, we have no set range or level of salary for the role of leader. Each person can determine how much income they make by how much of themselves they are willing to give. The more you give of yourself the more valuable you are to us and to those you will touch. We think this mindset about salary is one of the most important aspects of developing high performing leaders. Some of our leaders have told us they are so passionate about the opportunity to play the roles we allow them to play that they find greater financial benefit in how valuable they make others and the businesses they serve rather than how much salary they earn for themselves.

This view is shared by most of our leaders. Leaders such as this help us teach others leaders the real meaning of influence and passion. We will speak about influence a little later when we discuss important leadership competencies but for now we want you to visualize passion in this way because sometimes developing leaders misunderstand the difference between passion and emotion. Passion is always healthy and developing while emotions often can be destructive. Passion is a quality or character of uncommon leaders that is not expressed as are emotions but rather passion must be satisfied or fulfilled.

You see, it is by passion uncommon leaders do what they do for others and for their organizations and they do it well. Fulfillment of passion for the leader of uncommon effectiveness is perhaps what they look for most in terms of pay. Doing what they have grown to be passionate about and doing it well – that is to the uncommon leader greater than any salary we could offer.

Duty and Obligations: By now most of our developing leaders think, so what am I going to be doing? Well the answer is probably not as much of what you think and more than what you didn't think. A 2006 research study conducted by the University of Michigan's Ross School of Business examined how leaders spend their time. Results indicated that company performance increases when more time is spent on non-job roles.

Research data is below. In January 2006 – Dr. Theresa M. Welbourne from the Ross School of Business, University of Michigan and eePulse, Inc., released new research examining how leaders spend their time and how that time spent is associated with firm performance. Results indicate that by spending more time on what she calls *non-core job roles,* firms see higher levels of overall performance, especially firms with less than 500 employees. Respondents included 378 senior executives who participated in the bi-monthly, Leadership Pulse study. The basis for the study is a scientifically-validated method for assessing manager and leader performance based on five roles. These roles have been found to be critical for understanding overall, individual and firm performance and include:

- Job: Reflects the basic core job one is hired to perform and is often well described in the typical job description;
- Team: Reflects responsibilities for ongoing and project-based teams;
- Career: Includes responsibilities to enhance career and skills;

- Innovator: Covers work spent to develop new ideas, create new routines or improve on process;
- Organization Member: Reflects work done to support company overall, when it is not part of the other roles

The study indicates the average, overall percentages of time spent in each role from high to low as follows:

Job	45%
Team	16%
Career	8%
Innovator	19%
Organization	12%

The authors of the study say the average time spent by CEOs in particular in the job role, within a high performing company, is 36% versus 46% for the low performing firms. This is not surprising in that we know long-term competitive advantage comes from a workforce that is spending time doing things other than the 'core' job. If employees are focused only on the job, everything that your company does can be easily copied and replicated by your competitors. Long-term competitive advantage comes from the right combination of core job and non-core-job roles.

We believe research such as this is but the tip of things as far as success and how uncommon leaders spend their time. We do not prescribe for our leaders a list of duties and responsibilities you would commonly find in your typical organizations. We believe such lists actually limit what we expect our leaders should able to achieve with the people and organizations they are entrusted to lead. We expect the leaders to perform typical duties and responsibilities as they are necessary.

When staffing is needed they do this; when organizing is needed they do this; when budgeting is needed they do this too. But our leaders, leaders of uncommon effectiveness, are asked to spend the bulk of their time fulfilling the duty they have and the obligation they have to develop others and to develop the businesses they serve. We refer to it as their duty and their obligation because we understand before leaders can effectively do things to others they must fulfill a greater call to see it as their duty and their obligation to lead themselves well.

A sense of duty and obligation means more than performing tasks and responsibilities well; we expect no less of our leaders. A sense of duty and obligation means our leaders carry out their unassigned duty and obligation to be the best that can be (not the best that they can be) for others and for their businesses. This sense of duty and obligation will be necessary to serve the uncommon leader during times when challenges to individual performance are great.

To help leaders in our roles focus on their most important duty and obligations we prescribe four areas of duty that bring value to others beyond accomplishing tasks and value to the business beyond completing projects.

So given that we know with your talent and skills you must perform many duties and responsibilities typical of a leader to ensure things work efficiently, we will leave those to you to decide; we don't want to prescribe what you do with your hands.

But before the duties and responsibilities done with your talent and your hands are four areas of competence where it is your duty and your obligation to BE, KNOW and DO as a leader for those in the organizations and for the organizations you serve. These are to develop the competence to:

- Learn how to teach and to teach how to learn;
- Develop, build and guide your organizations;
- Model successful behaviors of uncommon people;
- Extend the depth and reach of what people can impact with their lives more than their roles and;
- Other duties as necessary for your people and the organizations to which you belong.

Learn How to Teach and Teach How to Learn

"Tell them they forget; show them and they remember; involve them and they learn".
Ben Franklin

At Dell Inc., Michael Dell (Chairman of the Board), and Kevin Rollins (President and CEO) both teach for several days in the top-level high-potential leadership-development programs and "leaders teaching leaders" is the predominant method of delivery of Dell's leadership programs. Steve Reinemund, Chairman and CEO of PepsiCo, is present during the entire week of Pepsi's senior high-potential program and teaches throughout. At UBS, The Group Executive Board (top 10 executives) mentor the next 60 executives below them (the Group Management Board or GMB), and the GMB mentor the next level below them. Both the GEB and the GMB actively and eagerly teach in UBS's top-level leadership-development programs.

What's going on here? Aren't university academic faculty supposed to be entrusted with the traditional role of teaching our corporate leaders? We don't believe so. It is the responsibility of academics to educate people and it is necessary to qualify our people in the skills and talents at the basic level of a role or position. But experience is what people gain when education is transformed from thoughts to action. This is what makes people successful in life; and this is the responsibility of the leader.

There is perhaps no greater impact the leader can have on people and on organizations than creating environments where people and the organizations are inspired to learn and to apply new things. The people of uncommon significance who fill our leadership roles all demonstrate a great capacity and competency to learn how to effectively teach others and to teach others how to learn. Teaching others is the default way uncommon leaders engage with others.

The speed and intensity of change in our environment is almost beyond the capability of people and organizations to react. Most people and business do not have the time to stay ahead of change because they are trying so desperately to keep up with change. Our leaders are required to create environments where our people and our organizations are able to learn from experiences they have yet to have. The uncommon leader doesn't spend his time telling others what to do; this is not teaching. No, the uncommon leader spends most of his time teaching others to find within themselves how to do things. When our leaders learn how to teach others and teach others how to learn we enjoy the benefits of:

Teaching and Learning Model

Benefit	People	Organization
Accountability	Learn to model behaviors and characters they expect to see in others	Perpetuates competencies that make the organization distinctively different from others
Capability	Learn to recognize and encourage use of untapped potential	Learns to become a stronger organization by integrating more individual and organizational capabilities
Succession	Learn to increase personal and professional value by identifying and closing developmental gaps	Sustains momentum by promoting the natural growth and progression of talent before critical needs actually develop
Collaboration	Teaches how to enhance teamwork among everyone	Learns to become team player to people and customers
Relations	Learns to develop trust among people	Learns to become trusted for what's best for customers and people

Becoming an uncommon leader requires you to get beyond simply telling others what to do; even the most immature leader can do that. By learning to teach others and teaching others to learn, the uncommon leader enlightens the hearts and the minds of others; they show others how to be successful within the framework and discipline of following a clearly delineated process; and they help others and the organization learn to go from working a job to fulfilling a passion.

Perhaps the greatest benefit of learning and teaching is found in creating impact beyond the role. *The uncommon leader is able to expand the impact of his leadership through the lives he touches directly into the lives he reaches indirectly.* Those who perform successfully in this role learn that teaching is how they engage others; values are how they express themselves with others; touching is how they impact others; reaching is how they expand impact with others and; developing / building is how they work with others.

One final thought on the principle of learning how to teach and teaching how to learn. The people most successful in our leadership roles are uncommon and different from good leaders in this way. Good leaders will spend most of their time immersed in telling and showing others how to do their jobs; they believe this is teaching. While the uncommon leaders in our roles spend their time showing others how to be successful in the role of the leader; they do not micromanage the job others are hired to do. They macro manage others by telling them about, showing them how and involving them in seeing their role as leader. We have found almost all people respond positively to this type of teaching by the uncommon leader.

Develop, Build and Guide Your Organizations

"What we are trying to do is build an organization that lasts, not to outlast the organization".
Footprints

In our leadership roles we ask our leaders to take on the responsibility of building organizations – not just running an organization. Great people build great organizations. Uncommon leaders do not use our organizations to simply act out their greatness. We find this approach too often with common leaders whose personal and professional statuses are greater than their organizations. Our leaders build strong lasting organizations with their greatness. In this way families are built stronger; marriages are stronger; boy scouts and girl scouts clubs are stronger; teams are stronger and businesses are stronger and more lasting.

People who want a leader role in our organizations must understand and be ready to live this principle. The value to our organizations is too great. We work diligently with our leaders to help them recognize and to overcome individual weaknesses that might translate into developing weak people or weak organizations. Don't be anxious however if you do not see our point right away. Remember we are here to help teach you how to learn so that you will learn how to teach others. Leaders in our programs focus on developing, building and guiding our organizations because in this they develop critical competencies such as self-awareness, self-control, decision-making, prioritizing and visioning.

It might seem to you at this point that in our list of the most important leader qualities everything is at the top. Well really it is not. We don't have a top leadership quality at the top of our quality list; we have a top leader perspective at the top of our leadership quality list. Leaders of uncommon effectiveness must have a perspective about the people they lead and the organizations they guide that is greater than the personal perspective they have for their own lives.

Every person touched by our leader; every person reached by our leader's leadership; every organization or business developed and guided by our leader must find within themselves the competencies and talents which they can use for producing great results. Too often we find good leaders overlook this important organizational building block. People and organizations can only achieve as much as is invested into them by the leader. Uncommon leaders rarely try to run organization to achieve what it is not yet designed or built to do.

We know many leaders new to our roles are often conflicted by this view. They see the organizations they are leading already developed and set on a particular course by the leader before them. Knowing that stopping the train and or returning to the station to start over is impractical and or impossible, how then, they often ask, does a person change the course and destination of a train that has already left the station and that has its destination already set?

The answer to this dilemma is uncommon at first glance but simple when it is understood. Leaders in this role learn that the most effective way to change the direction of a moving object, whether it is people or the businesses they lead, is to change the course and direction of the foundation on which people and the business must operate. Uncommon leaders don't work to change the direction of people or businesses per se, they work instead to change the direction of the road on which people and the business must travel.

As you get out ahead of where you want to go and reset the foundation the business will follow. The road and foundation consists of things like business values, vision, principles, services and so forth. The uncommon leaders who work in our programs have learned that the competence of building the organization is vital to mitigating the risks associated with running people and or the business at maximum speed and capacity over a system of tracks and rails not developed to support the speed, capacity and destination the business pursues.

Having a solid foundation is also critical to keeping people and the business on track and aligned. Good leaders, because they are singularly focused on getting the most out of people and or the businesses they operate, often unwittingly allow themselves to become driven by goals they set for themselves and or the business. Goals are important but without a solid foundation and environment in which they are pursued, goals can cause people to lose sight of what is important. And often people internalize goals differently than what the organization had in mind. My reason for completing your goal is different from your reason for assigning me that goal. With goals people and business often lose their direction because they are actually busy reading the map.

Leaders of uncommon effectiveness keep the big picture in focus. They do not permit themselves or those they serve to become distracted by the work they do. When you take a leader role in our organization you are expected to learn to think and to see that our people and the businesses in which they operate are part of the universe not the universe itself. Here is a little illustration to help you visualize the importance of the ability to see the bigger picture for your organization and the need for people to share not just the same goals but to share the same reasons for pursuing our goals.

The Three Stonecutters

One day a traveller, walking along a lane, came across three stonecutters working in a quarry. Each was busy cutting a block of stone. Interested to find out what they were working on, he asked the first stone cutter what he was doing. *I am cutting a stone!* Still no wiser the traveller turned to the second stonecutter and asked him what he was doing. *I am cutting this block of stone to make sure it is square and its dimensions are uniform so that it will fit exactly in its place in a wall.* A bit closer to finding out what they stonecutters were working on but still unclear, the traveller turned to the third stonecutter. He seemed to be the happiest of the three and when asked what he was doing replied, *I am building a cathedral.*

This story illustrates a key quality of our leaders – seeing a bigger picture and being driven by that vision. All three stonecutters were doing the same thing, but each gave a different answer. Each knew how to do his job but something set the third stonecutter apart from the others. We believe it was because the third stone cutter:

- Knew not just how and what to do but also knew why (Purpose);
- Viewed the whole not just his part (Values and Principles);
- Saw a vision – a sense of a bigger picture;
- Had the ability to see significance in work beyond the obvious (Values);
- Understood that a legacy lives on whether as the stone of a cathedral or in the impact made on others.

Leaders of uncommon effectiveness spend their time developing and building their organizations because they see the importance of the big picture. They develop the foundation of the organization because all the issues of people and the business flow from its foundation. When you take one of our roles as leaders we ask you to help people find greater purpose and meaning for their lives.

Peter Drucker in his book "The Practice of Management" uses this story to illustrate even further meaning:

- The first stonecutter said *I'm making a living*;
- The second stonecutter said *I'm doing the best job of stone cutting in the entire country* and;
- The third stone cutter said *I'm building a cathedral*.

In Drucker's version the first stone cutter knew what he wanted to get from his work; a fair day's work for a fair day's pay. The third stonecutter obviously had a positive attitude about his work perhaps because he saw the bigger picture. But what should we think about the second stonecutter? Drucker suggested this was a potential problem area. Here was someone focusing on his own narrow view of work, possibly to the detriment of a project as a whole. It is always dangerous when leaders allow or somehow encourage others to have a functional or professional sense of work at the expense of contributing to the whole organization.

Leaders in our programs learn to fight the natural tendency we have and that others may develop to allow work to become simply a means of earning a living; we fight the tendency to become focused on our individual performance or achievements and; we fight to instill a sense of the bigger picture for what we and the organizations are becoming.

Most of the time a person is awake is perhaps spent with us in our organizations and in our businesses doing the work they do for us. So we ask our leaders to focus on making that time as fulfilling as possible. It is worth the effort to us and to our people because people learn to work within the foundation of what makes our organizations strong and lasting; they learn to share a common vision and they learn to pursue goals that will keep them on track rather than to distract them.

So just what does it mean to develop the foundation of an organization? Well it means developing the:

- Purpose for which the organization exists;
- Values the organization holds and identifying the things the organization values and;
- Principles by which the organization will guide itself.

We will speak more with you about purpose, values and guiding principles when we cover with you the competencies our leaders require to perform uncommonly great in our roles. But for now we want to summarize our discussion of your responsibility to develop, build and guide people and organizations with this.

Years ago, when we were in the cathedral building business, it probably took many years, possibly over fifty in some instances, to build one cathedral. People who worked on these projects and leaders who led these efforts knew they were probably working on something that they would not see the end product in their lifetimes. Cathedrals are an incredible testament to our capacity as humans to accomplish incredible feats that would last for centuries.

How did they do this? How could they start with and stay with a task for so long and yet complete it with the perfection and marvel that we see in their work today? We believe an important part of the answer is that people then learned to have and to share a common vision. *We may not need many more cathedrals today but in our roles we are seeking leaders who have a view and perspective of greatness for the people they serve and the organizations they lead that will span beyond their lifetime.*

Do not be concerned that you may not be able to see things this way today. We are confident when you join our organization of uncommon leaders you will learn to see more than before; to see farther than before and to see faster than you have before.

Model Behaviors Uncommon to People

"Every man must decide whether he will walk in the light of creative altruism or in the darkness of destructive selfishness. Life's most persistent and urgent question is, what are you doing for others?"
Martin Luther King, Jr.

Modeling successful behaviors is the one aspect of duty and obligation that perhaps gives every leader their greatest challenge. It is so easy to be overcome in this area. Leaders of uncommon effectiveness must always be on guard for the challenges they will have in demonstrating great behavior. It is because behavior has such a tremendous impact on the leader's ability to establish a foundation of trust and confidence that we choose to make it one of our four most crucial and core elements of your duties. We take Dr. King's question to heart. We ask our leaders to always ask of themselves what good and positive things are they doing with their lives for others. For many people, one of the most frustrating aspects of life is not being able to understand other people's behavior.

Remember our discussion of the need for every leader to master the three self's in life: self-awareness, self-assurance and self-control. Self-control is the area of focus where destructive behaviors are born. Self-control is being able to keep behaviors and negative emotions and desires in check. Effectively demonstrating positive behaviors keeps others from having to manage around the leader's poor behaviors. Few leaders are able to achieve and maintain a consistent record of success when they allow destructive behaviors to rule how they engage with others.

Chapter Eight

In June 2009, the Harvard Business Review completed a study of more than 450 Fortune 500 executives focusing on what made the lowest performing executives fail. After reviewing the results from a detailed study of around 50 low performing executives they identified the 10 most common leadership shortcomings that lead to poor performance. It's important to note that each poor performing leader had at least one of these traits and most had several. Here they are:

- They lacked energy and enthusiasm. They rarely volunteer and fear being overwhelmed. One leader was described as having the ability to *suck all the energy out of any room;*
- They accept their own mediocre performance. They under promise and over deliver;
- They lack clear vision and direction. They believe their only job is to execute. Like a hiker who sticks close to the trail, they are fine until they come to a fork in the road;
- They have poor judgment. They make decisions that colleagues and subordinates consider not to be in the best interest of the organization;
- They don't collaborate. They avoid peers, act independently and view other leaders as competitors. As a result they are set adrift by the very people whose insights and support they need;

- They don't walk the talk. They set standards of behavior or expectations of performance and then violate them. They are perceived as lacking integrity;
- They resist new ideas. They reject suggestions from subordinates and peers. Good ideas aren't implemented and the organization gets stuck;
- They don't learn from mistakes. They may make no more mistakes than their peers but they fail to use setbacks as opportunities for improvement. They hid their errors or make excuses about them;
- They lack interpersonal skills. They make sins both of commission (they are abrasive and bullying) and omission (they are aloof, unavailable and reluctant to praise);
- They fail to develop others. They focus on themselves to the exclusion of developing others causing individuals and teams to disengage.

The common leaders among us look at these reasons for failure and say they are common sense. How could anyone behave this way and expect anything but failure? Well the answer is fairly simple. Man has a great capacity rationalize unacceptable behaviors as but minor distractions if any negative impact at all. And since they rationalize that everyone has some behavioral issue, it's all the same in the end; they are no different from anyone else. Ultimately people like this expect others to get along so we can move along.

Chapter Eight

At first many of our leaders do not understand why in our leader job roles we require it to be their duty to demonstrate positive leadership behaviors. They rightly think doing so should be common sense to everyone. But common sense is sometimes difficult for some to learn and to demonstrate; and common sense will always fall short of the sense of duty and obligation uncommon leaders demonstrate.

Let's take it that common sense simply means paying attention to the obvious or to what should be obvious; we know there is probably more to it than that but let's keep it as simple as we can for now. Let me illustrate how difficult it is for some people to act on what should be obvious.

Common Sense

A young medical student doing a rotation at a local Veterans Affairs (VA) hospital was assigned to work with other interns, patients and the attending physicians. One day on morning rounds the intern and another intern examined a patient with a black tongue. The patient had come in complaining of a severe cough and stomach irritation. The second intern researched all the causes of a black tongue and was eager to demonstrate his new knowledge to the attending physician later that morning.

When the physician arrived the intern started to lecture the physician and the patient. As he did this the physician interrupted him and asked the patient if he had used black cough drops to help his cold. The patient smiled and opened his pocket and took out a package of Smith Brothers black cough drops. The intern's face turned red with embarrassment as they all laughed. The intern was so focused on being a doctor that he forgot to ask a patient with what appeared to be a cold a very obvious question that any other person would have asked at that time.

When we review the Harvard Business Review research on reasons executives fail we realize that common sense is usually good sense only when you can see it, recognize it and apply it. Sometimes common sense can escape common sense in common people. We can agree on the surface the executives in their study perhaps sometimes did not use common sense in how they performed their duties and this probably contributed to their poor performance. But many executives probably didn't use common sense because they didn't recognize or perhaps didn't care about the lack of sense they made to others in their daily interpersonal interactions.

Uncommon leaders in our roles are asked to develop and to demonstrate a high level of self-awareness and self-control. We consider it the duty of any great leader to develop the self-awareness and self-control that leads to unquestionable behavior at all times. *Our leaders understand you cannot be an effective leader when you demonstrate ineffective behaviors.*

We don't want you to be too concerned at this point if you know you have struggled with little issues of behavior. The environment in which we create for our leaders will help you master what you need to master regarding your behavior. We are confident of that. All that is required of you is to acknowledge the duty and obligation you have personally to overcome negative behaviors and to have the will to change. Our leaders can help you do the rest. Let me illustrate a recent instance where a young leader learned to overcome a challenging behavior problem in the workplace.

Recently my second son was promoted to a leadership position in his business organization where he is now responsible for a small team of 12 people. One of his team leaders, perhaps the most competent one from a skill and talent perspective, was well liked and respected by her team but with one exception. When everything is going well with the team the team leader is at her best supporting them and enabling them to perform to a high level. But when the team is challenged with a problem, even the most minor of problems, the team leader becomes anxious, defensive and somewhat critical of team members. Her feelings and emotions are visibly shown in a change in her communication style.

When dealing with issues she talks louder than she does normally; her tone is more directive than normal; she points out blame and faults in others but never herself; and it stops being us and it becomes you. To the team leader she was simply doing what any leader must do to solve a problem. But to her team she takes on a critical nature that is often unnecessary; she is defensive to the point of making herself seem as if she is not a part of the team or the problem; and her tone of voice makes her appear to be condescending and disrespectful of others.

After talking with my son about the issue we decided he would do two things to help her become more aware of how her behavior is perceived by her team. Of course we anticipated that speaking with her about her issue would lead to a manifestation of her problems. So before dealing with her on what was sure to be a negative issue my son watched and recorded how she dealt with her team on positive issues. Her actions and behaviors were great.

On the day he spoke to her about how she deals with negative issues she of course became defensive; she raised her voice and she spoke of how people didn't do what they were supposed to do. When my son shared with her the video recording of how she responded under positive circumstances and she compared that to how she responded to him on a negative issue only then was she able to see the obvious difference in her behavior.

It was clear to her and my son that her reactions when faced with negative issues had more to do with a lack of self-awareness, lack of self-control, and her own personal insecurities each of which together contributed to her behaving in a self-serving uncaring manner. Was my son able to help this young leader improve her behavior? Yes! He did that by helping her to see and to accept that just as importantly as it was for her team to perform to a high level, it was equally important and in fact her duty and obligation to overcome the personal issues that hindered her effectiveness and in the end the effectiveness of the team.

Great behaviors help develop environments of harmony, trust and respect for one another. Our leaders are expected to behave in ways so that their maturity is always greater than their chronological age. Bad behaviors and habits are unfortunately a part of life. We don't typically like to focus on what is wrong to get at what is right. The leaders in our programs know that just because a person knows what not to do does not mean that person knows what to do. But with the issue of behaviors it is helpful to point out poor behaviors when they happen so that our leaders can have a better chance to recognize the subtle ways negative habits can creep into lives.

A Business Week article lists the following 15 interesting bad habits, complied by executive coach Marshall Goldsmith, describing what hinder leaders from progressing in their organizations:

- Winning too much: The need to win at all costs and in all situations—when it matters, when it doesn't, and when it's totally beside the point;

- Adding too much value: The overwhelming desire to add our two cents to every discussion;
- Passing judgment: The need to rate others and impose our standards on them;
- Making destructive comments: The needless sarcasms and cutting remarks that we think make us sound sharp and witty;
- Starting with "No," "But," or "However": The overuse of these qualifiers, which secretly say to everyone, "I'm right. You're wrong;"
- Telling the world how smart we are: The need to show people we're smarter than they think we are;
- Speaking when angry: Using emotional volatility as a management tool;
- Withholding information: The refusal to share information in order to maintain an advantage over others;
- Claiming credit we don't deserve: The most annoying way to overestimate our contribution to any success;
- Making excuses: The need to reposition our annoying behavior as a permanent fixture so people excuse us for;
- Clinging to the past: The need to deflect blame away from ourselves and onto events and people from our past; a subset of blaming everyone else;
- Playing favorites: Failing to see that we are treating someone unfairly;

- Refusing to express regret: The inability to take responsibility for our actions, admit we're wrong, or recognize how our actions affect others;
- Passing the buck: The need to blame everyone but ourselves;
- An excessive need to be "me": Exalting our faults as virtues simply because they exemplify who we are.

We don't want you to feel like our leaders are perfect and always demonstrate positive behaviors. They are not. But what is perfect about the uncommon leader is the desire they have to always be mindful of and to watch for in themselves the seeds of poor behavior. We believe like them, you will come to accept the personal and professional accountability to represent all that it really means to be an uncommon leader for your family; for your teams; and for your organizations and businesses. It is in the battles we have within ourselves that the great competencies of courage, selflessness, respect, disciplined behavior and consistency are born. You will find each of these traits is among most desired traits of any leader.

So as you fulfill your duty and your obligation to demonstrate positive behaviors and as you teach other leaders to do the same things, learn to develop a greater sense of self-awareness and of self-control. Leaders who are disciplined and aware of the impact they have on others have learned to follow purpose rather than to be pulled by desires. Here is what I mean:

A Model for Successful Behaviors

Follow purpose	Pulled by desires
Follow a vision	Pulled by goals
Take a journey	Seeks a destination
Move by passion	Give in to negative emotion
React through values	Reacts to circumstances
Build homes	Builds houses
Are ruled by character	Ruled by problems
Are driven	Pulled
Are held accountable	Holds others accountable

Chapter Eight

Leader Role Requirements / Qualifications

"Enter through the narrow gate. For wide is the gate and broad is the road that leads to destruction, and many enter through it. But small is the gate and narrow the road that leads to life and only a few find it."
Matthew 7:13-20

Well we have finally come to the point of describing the fundamental requirements and qualifications we have for your role as a leader with us. We do not have cut in stone job requirements or qualifications for any of our leader positions. Uncommon leaders have learned you can't adequately predict the success of a leader by simply looking at years of functional experience, college degrees, professional certifications and or things like past accomplishments. Things such as these are but one dimension of what it ultimately takes for our leaders to achieve consistently high levels of success.

But long before a person is picked out to be a leader they usually have begun to stand out for the qualities we find in most successful people. So we won't prescribe specific job requirements for leaders that only some people can achieve; we describe leadership potential that anyone who is willing, can learn to perfect. Our areas of potential are found in the blend and integration of traits found in the personal, professional and social dimensions uncommon leader.

Goleman's describes the usefulness of his components of Emotional Intelligence (EI) as a form of intelligence that goes a long way in describing what separates smart people from leaders. He believes it is hard to find a successful leader who does not or is not described by an uncommon sense of self-awareness, self-regulation, motivation, empathy and or social skills. Like Goleman, we believe the uncommon leaders in our programs demonstrate a special blend of and presence of potential in:

- Personal Dimension
    - Purpose
    - Courage
    - Uncommon maturity
- Social Dimension
    - Respect
    - Empathy
    - Commitment
- Professional Dimension
    - Sense of Duty
    - Dependability
    - Aptitude

We believe as you develop your potential in these areas you place yourself on the path to becoming the leader of uncommon effectiveness. The path may seem narrow and too restrictive for some to believe they can find success along the way. But the reality is that the straight and narrow path is the easier and most beneficial path to follow because our leader learns to discipline their walk and to overcome things that would distract them when following a broader path.

Many people view potential with skepticism. Too often they believe potential does not develop into the results they desire. Instead they prefer to trust in past performance and skill qualifications, or aptitude as the best indicators of future success. But past performance and skills can never be indicators of the courage you display; or the purpose by which you are driven; or the empathy by which you engage with others; or the sense of duty by which you operate. And each of these things is a critical element in achieving and sustaining uncommon leadership effectiveness.

We must consider past performance and skill but we must not overlook the weightier personal and social dimensions of the person of the leader. Do not be discouraged that we may appear to be complicating the simple route to identifying the job qualifications of a leader. We are not complicating but simplifying matters so that you and all others will have great clarity around what it takes to become a leader of uncommon effectiveness.

Remember, we view the role of a leader apart from the person of a leader. Aptitude, skills and job experiences are rightly associated with the position of a leader; they are the outward signs of the skills required for success in a position. It is a part of the leader's organizational development responsibility to clearly specify position requirements. We typically do this well, a degree in this, three years of this, experience in this area and so forth. This is the basis of how we match people skills to each position.

But how we choose leaders from among people should be different. We cannot make it a priority to look at skills and experiences for these alone will limit the pool of potential leaders available to us. We must look at the more significant and impactful qualities of a leader that are almost always associated with the person. These qualities are more inward than outward; they are more experiences than achievements.

And these qualities are rightly identified as areas of personal and social competence. Where skills and experiences may tell you what a person should be capable of doing, personal and social competencies will tell you how well and the level of effectiveness a person should achieve using their skills.

Let me illustrate how you get from an area of potential to an uncommon outcome using the competency model below:

Leader Competency Model

Potential Attribute	Description	Manifested Outcome
Purpose	The reason for our being; being driven and not pulled	Decisiveness, Vision, Integrity, Clarity, Focus and Wisdom
Courage	The ability to act when fear says don't	Overcomer, Achievement Motivation, Confidence, Selflessness, and Resilience
Uncommon maturity	Wisdom to see with the heart what others miss with their eyes	Judgment, Fearlessness, Experience
Respect	Acknowledging the value of others and of authority	Trust, Value and Influence
Empathy	Considerate of others	Connects / in touch with others, Trust and Belief
Commitment	A sense of reliability driven from within	Loyalty, Honesty, and Integrity
Sense of duty	The self-imposed obligation to fulfill all expectations	Self-accountable, Reliable, Selfless and Achievement
Dependability	Doing what is expected of oneself	Trust, Confidence and Consistency
Aptitude	Knowing what to do and how to do it	Excellence, Skillful, Professionalism and Success

Chapter Eight

Our leader job announcement is almost complete and ready to be posted. Our description of uncommon leader qualifications is designed to stir up your desire to become the best leader you can be. Leadership is more mindset than positional. This mindset is so uncommon and so different that when people see it in people we are often unable to adequately describe it. And often if we see the mindset in someone we do not associate with being a leader or someone whom we do not believe will become a leader, we tend to overlook the importance of what the mindset means.

Every great and effective leader has this mindset. It is a heart of the person given to something other than the person himself. It is a commitment to discovering and living for yourself how great you can be and then teaching others how to live in their greatness.

During one of our development programs in 2010, I met a lady named Dana. Dana was one of about 20 participants in this executive development seminar. Over the course of the two day seminar it was clear to me as it was to others taking the seminar that Dana was uncommonly good. She walked to a different beat; sang a different tune; sought and achieved greater objectives.

In a private moment during one of our breaks, I asked Dana how she had learned to be as successful as she was. She thought only for a moment and replied *I learned how to really be successful in the things I do only after I first learned how to be successful with the person I am.* She told me for many years because she didn't manage herself well she defeated all her potential and all her chance for greatness. It was when she decided to change her mindset and determined to be great with the person she was within that she was able to become greater with the person we see outwardly.

Helping people learn to tap into their abilities to be greater than they are today is the greatest natural gift we have in life. Like Dana, we can create the path to greatness for ourselves, if only we know how to take control. Our view is similar to Dana's. We teach uncommon leadership principles because we want a world that is uncommonly great. If we are led by average leaders we have an average world; average homes; average marriages and average businesses. But average is not for us and we hope you will come to reject average for yourself.

It is the leader in each of us – that inner person who says to us inwardly – you are meant to be greater than you are. When we get to know ourselves better, when we get to know our abilities better, then we are able to be and do better in ways to bring profound impact beyond our roles. It's the leader in us that drives us in this way. The uncommon leader is clear about who they are, what they are capable of doing and how to make a difference. They know how to align all they are to roles and opportunities to bring profound impact in what they do. They are uncommon spouses, uncommon parents, uncommon teachers and uncommon people of business.

The leader in us sees the challenge differently. As did Dana, they see the challenge is to conquer something within and to teach others how to do the same thing. When that battle is won they are freed to walk in an inner sense of success that spills over into all the practical things they do in life. They model great behavior because they have conquered poor behavior within themselves. They insist on behaving great for you and for me and they are driven to teach others how to do it. They are authentic in every way and because of this they seemingly enjoy fulfilled lives.

    Their satisfaction comes from what they are giving not from what they are receiving. When you have contact with an uncommon leader of this mindset you will be naturally challenged to move from what is good to what is great; to move from what is great to what is uncommon and to be ready to move from what is uncommon to what is yet described for you as a person.

    The uncommon leader seemingly invents and reinvents hisself constantly as they walk the journey of development. They act like leaders in every aspect of their lives because they are leaders first. They don't just act like a leader because of a role they play; they don't just work like a leader; they are leaders who live and work to uncommon levels of greatness. You can be this too!

    Uncommon leaders in our programs have awakened to and have overcome a challenge that keeps most people down. They see clearly each of us has within us the seeds of greatness and that to release the power of those seeds to grow we need only to stop learning to be weak. We must stop learning to work around instead of working out our weaknesses; stop learning to give in to our desires instead of pursuing our purpose for life. In business the uncommon leader of this mindset becomes more than trusted partners to their business clients and customers; they become more than trusted partners to their vendors. They become the key resource, the most valuable resource their clients, their customers and their vendors use to achieve their objectives because clients and customers and vendors all believe the leader has their best interests at heart.

Realize that you are fearfully and wonderfully made; you have no shortcoming that cannot be overcome. You are destined to do and to be great things for those you love and care about, for those you live and work with and for those you find the joy and relaxation of spending leisure time with. Awake to the greatness that was created in you, even as your birth itself is a miraculous thing, and stop learning to be weak.

Let me finish our job announcement for the uncommon leader in you by sharing a story with you that will illustrate the power of leading in uncommon ways; of awakening to the power of living in our strengths and of the failure that comes when we live in personal and professional weaknesses.

There were two prostitutes who lived together. No one else lived with them. Over the course of time they both became pregnant about the same time. They both gave birth to sons just a few days apart. One night in the first few days after the birth of their sons one prostitutes carelessly smothered her son while they slept at night. When she realized what she had done she quickly switched her dead son with the live son of the other prostitute under cover of darkness.

When day came the other prostitute went to feed her child she found instead the dead child of her roommate. When confronted the roommate claimed that the child that lived was hers. When the two of them could not resolve the issue between them they took their problem and the live child to the King.

The prostitute whose child it was spoke first. She explained to the King that the other prostitute had smothered and killed her son and had switched the dead child for her living son during the night. The other prostitute denied this of course and said that the son that lived was hers. The King, not having any witness or any other facts to consider in helping him to make a decision, asked for a sword. When the sword was brought to the king he commanded that the live child be split into two halves with one half being given to each woman.

Well the prostitute whose child it was stopped the king and told him to give the child (her child) to the other prostitute. She reasoned it was better that the child live with someone who wasn't the real mother than to be killed. The other prostitute told the king to go ahead and split the child; she reasoned that if she couldn't have him then neither should the woman whose child it was have him. The king considered what the women said and then made the decision to give the child to the woman who was willing to give up the child. The king knew the child had to belong to the woman who would give him up because love never agrees with death.

Many people who know this story think of the great wisdom the king demonstrated that day. In fact the king became known for his wisdom throughout the land for how he handled this incident. He was uncommon and the uncommon leader always sees more than others. But not much is ever said about the prostitutes. Nothing was written about their lives and the choices they made that day. But one of them, the one whose child it really was, learned to live in uncommon strength that day and the other failed in her weakness. The real mom, instead of giving in to being selfish, as did the other prostitute, rose to become selfless; instead of taking as did the other prostitute, she gave; instead of giving in to her desires as did the other prostitute, she was moved by purpose of life.

She learned at that moment to stop living weak and to live strong. When everything about the situation said fight for what is yours, she decided to fight for someone and for something that couldn't fight for itself - the child and the opportunity to have and to live a great life of his own. And she won! This is what living in the greatness of uncommon leadership is all about. We want our leaders to learn to give themselves to achieving what is best for their homes; what is best for their spouses; in business what is best for their customers; and in all settings they seek what is best for others by seemingly denying what is best for them.

We are prepared to make you an offer of a position with us right now. We hope you will accept the offer of a role as a leader of uncommon greatness with our organization. We are always looking to add people like you. And if you don't feel like you are qualified for the role just remember that we don't specify position requirements that limit anyone; we describe competencies that live in each of us usually as untapped potential. All we ask of you is to agree with us to take the journey to live the potential for greatness that you have already. When you do this you will develop:

- A desire to do a good work for others and for the businesses you serve – We have enough misleading that is harmful to people and destructive to businesses;
- The disposition to place the good of others ahead of personal good – Self-interest is never the best interest;
- The ability to learn and to teach – It's how we perpetuate great things done by great people;
- A chaste behavior – Behavior that stands out for its goodness rather than sticks out for its weakness;
- Knowledge beyond limits – You don't have to know everything but must know what you ought to know;
- To live a life of purpose – Driven by purpose of heart not by material desires;
- To be more value to others and to your employers than costs – Never seeking all you deserve and always delivering more than what is expected;
- The ability to connect with others – Always put more into relationships than what you take;
- The know how to get things done – Always reject your marginal efforts and inspect what you expect from yourself;
- Ability to make things better – Empty yourself of your best and others will reward you with their best.

Chapter Eight

Our job announcement will remain posted until every person who wants to develop an uncommon capacity to do well has had the opportunity to work with us. Our competitors will continue to offer positions to you that on the surface offer the hopes of great short term gains, but in reality they are the broad path and the wide road to mediocre achievements in the long term. Unfortunately many people are fooled by them and take their offer of a broad way and a wide path to great success only to find that at the end they are worse off than they were at the start.

At first glance our offer seems like it is more difficult because we ask you to deal first effectively with yourself and then with others. This is the way of success for the leader of uncommon significance; the doorway seems narrow and the pathway seems too straight for those who live by the quick desires of the heart. But for the people who find and use this path come consistent and indescribable success beyond their lifetime. There is an uncommon leadership role for everyone in any position and for everyone in places everywhere. It's your time to step up and follow the Footprints of those on the path to uncommon significance!

During my work with business executives we typically encourage each executive to have a personal relationship with a creditable coach and mentor. Every successful person would benefit from having the consistent relationship with someone who can provide external insight into their growth and development. We created the Footprints model of leadership so that it can be used as a personal or business leadership coach and mentor. This approach ultimately serves to train skills but to grow leaders. There are several things unique to a healthy leadership mentoring and development environment:

- Principles of Leadership: we start with a foundation built on principles of effective leadership;
- The Leadership Oath: *First, never be deceived by yourself*;
- The Learning Model: We follow a model of learning captured in this quote by Ben Franklin – *Tell me and I forget; show me and I remember; involve me and I learn;*
- The First Person Led: We help you learn to lead more effectively the *First Person*;
- The Growth Model: We establish and follow a leadership effectiveness model that simplifies your development and growth as an effectiveness leader;
- Leadership Dynamics: We help you blend the dynamics of leadership characteristics, traits and skills with people and business into more effective personal and professional leadership;
- Challenges to Effective Leadership: Footprints helps to identify and to overcome challenges that inhibit developing effective leadership.

Developed to Last

"So the abundance will be unknown in the land because of that subsequent famine; for it will be very severe".
Genesis 41:30-31

Uncommon development results

The uncommon leader usually adopts a language and an environment of leadership that reflects the rapid nature of change and the impact change has on the long term success of people and businesses. People are developed for long term success more than just the task at hand; businesses are developed to deliver enduring greatness more than to survive the current crisis. Sometimes common leaders allow themselves, their businesses and people to forget how difficult things were because they are enjoying how great things are. Then at other times in enjoying how great things are they sometimes fail to adequately plan and prepare for successes they need tomorrow.

Remember we are a fast-paced transaction driven world that seeks issues focused common type leadership. This is the prevailing norm in almost every part of our society. But it actually works to hinder the full development of our people, our societies and our businesses.

The common leader manages people and their businesses to survive; but the uncommon leader develops people and their businesses to last!

Footprints   **Chapter Nine**   Developed to Thrive
                                  Not Just to Survive

Where common leadership is developed to respond to specific issues, the uncommon leader is developed fully and completely to bring comprehensive impact through change. They are developed for unseen challenges, to do what skills and talents have not been asked to do yet.

Common leaders are generally expected to be good at the one thing they do well. Because people are more difficult to lead today and because change happens faster than business leaders can react, we have begun to develop leaders to just get by. Businesses and individuals have grown to accept and even embrace the notion that people can get by with a less than fully developed set of competencies.

One example of a commonly accepted business practice should help you understand what I mean. It is almost common place now in businesses to embrace the idea of hiring two people with complementary skills to do the job of one person. I often work with executive leaders of businesses who may have personal weaknesses or they may have leaders who are weak in one or more critical area. But this leader may be the best person the business has for knowing what and how to do some things critical to driving short term success (remember, those who know what and how will always have a place). These businesses sometimes opt to work around the weaknesses of that person by hiring another person who has a complimentary skill set. It's the good buy bad guy approach to managing.

Chapter Nine
Developed to Thrive Not Just to Survive

By managing around fully developing the leader we have developed the idea that we can put together a team of people who represent all the competence necessary for success of the team. In reality though what we do is put together a team of weak people who are not developed to last but rather developed to survive the short term. Weak leaders will inevitably lead or produce weak teams.

When we operate this way we learn work within our weaknesses rather than from a position of strength. We do not fully develop our ability to use the full range of competencies and skills we will need as individuals or as businesses to maintain long term success over time. An uncommon leader would reject this notion and take the steps necessary to fully develop themselves. *Skills are necessary to get you a place on the team but competencies are needed to earn you a spot in the game.* We need both to be fully successful.

Here is a visual of what I mean by the need for both skills and competencies:

Leadership Skills and Competencies

Skills	Competencies
Indicate what you can do	Demonstrates how well you do things
Identifies your qualifications	Qualifies your impact
Sets you apart from those who can't	Sets you above those who can
Describes scope of capabilities	Broadens and deepens impact of your capabilities
The measure of your abilities	The ability to bring measured impact

Because we have regressed (some would say this idea is actually progress) to this point, we have actually developed a society of weak leaders leading weak organizations trying to achieve uncommon greatness. The quote above – said another way – seven years of great feast and abundance will be totally forgotten by seven years of comparable famine because the famine will be so great. When we fail to fully develop all of who we are and what we need to be effective, we fail to develop cognitive abilities such as wisdom, insight and intuition which are needed to guide and temper our desires. We make poor decisions that in the short term appear to be beneficial but in reality they are detrimental to our long term success.

Here is an example of what I mean. Lots of plants and vegetables have what is called a taproot system. The taproot is the primary root for a plant; from it the life of every other root is sustained with nutrients. Farmers and gardeners know to preserve the taproot if you want to preserve the plant; or vice versa, you find and destroy the taproot when you want to destroy a whole plant.

The taproot looks much like any other root on the plant so it takes a trained eye to spot them. The taproot of a vegetable such as a carrot or a potato looks much like the edible carrot or potato we harvest. You must be careful not to harvest the taproot or you destroy the ability of the carrot or potato to produce more vegetables.

Many people and many businesses, focused on the short term need for food or revenue growth, will unwisely harvest the taproots of plants, customers, vendors or partner relationships getting short term gain but destroying long term capability to produce more in the future. This happens because people have not fully developed their wisdom, insight and the ability to look beyond the immediate to the future. The short term success they achieve and enjoy actually put them on a path to failure.

When we are not fully developed, we are unable to appreciate a natural law that says all that is possible to us may not be beneficial to us; many things may be permissible to us but not all permissible things make us better. The leader of uncommon effectiveness resists the growing tendency to develop people for greatness in one dimension rather than to develop the greatness the whole person. A half knowledgeable farmer probably is not going to be a very successful farmer over time.

A weak manager would welcome the idea of having a person of opposite skill or competence work together to offset a personal or professional weakness; it allows the weak manager to keep his job while continuing to move safely through the organization. A weak leader, if he is a leader at all, would reject off hand the idea of having another person work to offset a leadership weakness but they still may not work to fully develop themselves. But uncommon leaders reject their own marginal efforts before they reject the efforts of others. They look to develop themselves to be fully capable to excel at all aspects of leading and performing successfully in the roles they play. Leaders of uncommon effectiveness know their own weaknesses; they are driven to work and to improve themselves, often doing it at their own expense and on their own time.

Each of us is meant to be a variable and not a constant in our journey through life. We change the things around us as we develop and evolve. Scientists established long ago that the world was not linear; rather it is complex and somewhat chaotic. So is the institution of the family; our schools; social organizations and our businesses. The environments in which we must operate are by nature dynamic; they cannot be as predictable as a trip through a drive through window. The language and approach we take to leading effectively must adapt to the unpredictable and chaotic world in which leaders must lead and in which people must develop and where businesses must perform.

Remember the uncommon leader must develop fully his personal, social and professional dimensions of leading; they are necessary to for the whole person. Accomplishments are always soon forgotten because the famine for more comes back again and again and stronger each time. *People will remember the experiences of an uncommon leader long after they have forgotten the results achieved.* That is what it means to be developed to last. Both the person and the experience of the person live on in the lives of others long after the leader has moved on.

The uncommon leader's path to success is lined with many incredible accomplishments and unforgettable experiences. Why is this so? Because the uncommon leader develops and operates within an environment that nurtures and develops people to be more than just a slice of the pie; each person is challenged to never stop developing who they are to BE; to never stop growing and learning the things they need to KNOW and to never stop challenging themselves to perfect the things they need to DO. *Lasting results come from efforts that last continually.*

Working out Development

Integrating and perfecting development is the second element of being developed to last. This is the output element; what the person does with the development received. It is a function primarily of the degree to which a person has the self-will to transform knowledge into a perfected skill. Uncommon leaders are driven by an insatiable will to be better, to know better and to perform better – not better than others – but better than they were the day before. And because they drive themselves this way and they know it is a key component of being successful, they have learned to inspire others to transform their knowledge into perfected skill levels that are uncommon.

John Maxwell published a book "Talent is Never Enough". The core of what Maxwell says in his book is simple. Talent alone, your talent, is not enough to make you a greater more successful person than you are. Talent makes you proficient at what you do but it doesn't make you do great things with your talent. That requires a heavy dose of will, commitment, devotion and dedication to perfecting. The uncommon leader knows that talent alone is insufficient to bring a high level of consistent results. So he helps others learn how to reach within themselves to challenge and perfect uncommon ways of thinking so that acts and habits and personal development uncommon to them before would become common place.

Chapter Nine

Developed to Thrive Not Just to Survive

My first day in the Army is one day I will never forget. I left home early that morning a young 17 year old kid who thought he knew everything. I was going to become a soldier. Later that same day after arriving at the Military Entrance Processing Station (MEPS for short) in South Carolina, my transformation from civilian life to soldier began. The Army realizes that it is easier to teach a soldier who was once a civilian to perform to the level of a leader than it is to teach a person who still thinks like a civilian to become a great soldier.

So they cut my hair; they issued me a uniform and some boots and; they even gave me a new name – Lieutenant. This was done for many reasons but one reason stood out to me. The Army wanted me to transform the way I thought about myself; they wanted me to identify with what I was to become not what I was before.

The Army doesn't have a name for it but us Lieutenants created our way of looking at it. We called this "Monkeys do what monkeys do"! What we mean is simple. We can teach monkeys to do a number of things humans do; eat from a plate; use a toilet; type on a keyboard and so forth. But if you leave a monkey to roam about your home all day while you are at work you are likely to return to find that the monkey has reverted to doing what monkeys do. Unless you are able to transform the monkey and give it a new perspective it is likely to always return to doing what monkeys naturally do.

Chapter Nine

Developed to Thrive Not Just to Survive

Uncommon leaders know that to achieve and to sustain effectiveness over time they must first transform how they think of themselves – they have to see themselves as leaders and then they develop themselves to be effective in the roles leaders must play. They internalize development to transform themselves into someone they were not yesterday; it isn't enough to just add new talents and skills to the person they have always been.

Our military has a unique environment for developing leaders that is almost impossible to duplicate. Every service man or woman is developed to lead. Each service has an institution responsible for developing the components of a consistent leadership development process. Each service funds development of its leaders because leaders are critical to the success of the service mission. Each service has a closed environment where turnover of service members is fairly low and very predictable. Each service member is obligated by contract to remain in the service for a specific amount of time therefore the services can target more development and training at each person and it can expect to reap the benefit.

Each service member learns to speak the same leadership language because the development process is consistent. In this environment service members develop the will to perfect knowledge and skills. But there is a key. Service members are not all expected to think the same things; they are all expected to think the same way. By this I mean service members are transformed to think of themselves within the context of what is best for our country; they are asked to use their lives to make a difference. This drives the way their acts and habits and their very characters of persons are developed. Their hearts are shaped to desire what is best for others before seeking what is best for them. So they enjoy great effectiveness in developing themselves.

Unfortunately outside of our services these positives are challenges that are difficult to reproduce and or to overcome in other settings. Developing people with a sense of selfless duty for their families, their teams, their organizations or their businesses is difficult because people are not exposed to a consistent environment where this behavior is consistently demonstrated. Unlike the services, leaders in business may come and go almost as they please. This puts a tremendous level of strain on the organization to develop and keep a consistent focus.

With each change in a significant business leader there may well be a corresponding change in the overall culture and environment in the organization. In the corporate world, people join businesses for different reasons. They do not always share the vision of the business and they are not always aligned with the business in the direction it is going. Even in homes or in social organizations people ultimately are motivated and inspired by different things. Unlike the Army where everyone is expected to be a soldier and former civilian; in the business or in social settings professionals identify with their work more so than with the business where they work.

While it could be argued that it rightly should be this way, it creates a powerful conflict of will for the individual and for the organization. Each individual has personal and professional desires that may or may not align with what the business needs a person to desire most. And while a business use of pay and other incentives are designed to motivate an individual to give his or her best, external motivations are insufficient to bring about the change of heart necessary we are speaking of here.

The uncommon leader behaves in ways and does some things that are uncommonly effective at developing environments to challenge the heart and will of others to make a difference. The uncommon leader gets at the heart of others by:

- Improving how they think - thinking powerfully but acting selflessly;
- Improving how they act – acting selflessly but performing professionally and;
- Improving how they perform – Performing professionally but driven to always making a difference.

Chapter Nine

Making a Difference

One day a wise man working from his balcony on a beach saw what appeared to be a young man walking and then dancing along the beach. For several days the wise man saw this young man return to the same area of the beach where he walked and danced to and from the edge of the water. Curious the wise man decided to go down one morning and ask the young man about what he was doing.

As he approached the young man he noticed that he wasn't dancing at all. Instead the young man was bending over and picking up something from the sand and running to the water to throw it in. Even more curious now the wise man hurried to speak to the young man. As the wise man approached the young man he called out gently *young man, what are you doing*? The young man stopped, turned to the wise man and said *why I'm throwing starfish into the ocean.*

The wise man stood still and said *young man why are you throwing starfish into the ocean? Did you look at the beach? There are miles and miles of beach and starfish are all over. You can't possibly make a difference.* The young man bent over, took another starfish, jogged over to the edge of the ocean and gently tossed the starfish into the ocean beyond the breaking waves. As the young man walked back to the wise man he pointed over his shoulder and said *made a difference to that one.*

The wise man was ashamed. He turned and walked back to his cottage. For the next few days he pondered what he had learned from that young man's actions. Finally the wise man understood. He has missed the essential message in what the young man was doing. So many of us he thought go through life missing the essential meaning of it all. We have two choices. We can go through life by taking in all that we can or we can live life by giving all that we can to make a difference.

Teaching others how to make a difference with their lives is perhaps one of the most powerful ways to inspire others to achieve beyond their dreams. People such as this are those who are developed to last. They produce results that last longer than the common person. They produce experiences that are not quickly forgotten and the organizations to which they belong are built to last beyond the most recent accomplishment.

Planning Your Success Successfully

"If you don't know where you are going, you will end up someplace else". Yogi Berra, widely quoted sports legend.

Effective organizational development and planning is perhaps the most overlooked and yet the most important competence a leader must develop. In our business we integrate organizational development planning with executive development because we know how important one is to the other. Not too long ago people used to diet in efforts to control their weight; now we know weight control requires a lifestyle of changes that include complimentary components of diet, exercise and physical fitness and so on. So in much the same way we see planning and organizational development as components critical to effective leadership.

Uncommon leaders are natural planners or they should be; they know that developing the organization and planning are evidences that effective leadership is flourishing. A leader who does not or who cannot plan well is likely to be a weak leader who cannot execute well. We see this type of apathy toward organizational development and planning in businesses almost every day. It is the one area of leader development where there is the greatest push back in the need to change behaviors. Mention plans and business people tend to think time spent and time wasted sitting on your hands. The idea of a plan seems limiting to them; they have been successful because they learned to act quickly and decisively. Circumstances, they think, don't wait to ask if you have a plan before you are required to take action.

I typically see three types of inadequate planners in our most critical personal, social and business roles today. The poor leaders do not plan well because they are reacting to what happened yesterday; good leaders don't plan well because they are busy solving the problems that happened today and; great leaders do not plan well because they are caught up in the short term focus trap where results are needed and they are needed tomorrow.

If you do not know where you are going how will you know what road to take; how will you know what competencies you must develop; how will you know what training is needed and how will you communicate to others what you want to do?

Failing to develop a strong organization and planning its success is core to the problems leaders have in learning to execute effectively today. Leaders often get ahead of their organizations, their businesses and even their families and ask them to do things they are not yet prepared to do because of the lack of a plan and the short term focus on results.

Uncommon leaders rarely make this critical mistake. You see, when they took on the role of leader they had in their hangars both a 747 jet plane and a NASA Space Shuttle. Both planes can fly but only one can travel to the moon and back. And though they have aircraft in their hangars, the uncommon leader does not even assume that air travel is the way they should approach their transportation needs. They take the time to assess the organization as a whole to determine what it is capable of doing, what it can do well today and they consider that against plans for the future of the organization. The 747 just might be appropriate for their needs since a trip to the moon is not one of their priorities.

By taking time to assess needs and desires, they are able to focus on key activities that will help develop the organization for future success. These activities include identifying:

- The Plan for Success – Creating the plans that will guide the future actions of the business;
- Values - identifying values of the organization and distinguishing between the values the business holds and the things the business values;
- Purpose - Determining the inherent purpose of the business and it's reason for being;
- Principles – Identifying the principles of rule which will guide how people and the business will operate;
- Vision – identify the vision of what the future possibilities are for the business by clarifying and setting direction;
- Direction - Identifying the direction the business will take to embark on its vision which includes:
    o Determining objectives or missions and;
    o Developing goals and;
- Organizational Competencies – Identifying areas of the business where the organization can be the "best" at doing.

Chapter Ten

Understanding needs and desires is critical to developing the discipline to plan your success. It would be foolish to try to fly a 747 to the moon just because you have desire but no need to do that. Likewise it would be a waste to use a NASA Space Shuttle for your local or routine transportation needs when an automobile would be sufficient for your business. The point I'm making is this. Leaders have become so preoccupied with goal setting that is a reaction to short term unplanned and unvetted desires that they put goal setting ahead of solid objective organizational planning and development. They fail to use the strength of the organization in the most effective way and they fail to realize the impact weaknesses in the organizations will have on achieving organizational goals.

In our business, we are confronted continually with businesses on the brink of failure because they have great goals they could not and did not plan to accomplish. Setting goals is the tail end of a thorough process of planning the future of an organization, developing the organization to perform at a high level and then setting goals for accomplishments you want the organization to achieve over time. Goals are the place where you end after you have developed the plan, trained and developed the organization, bought the plane and developed priority objectives for your future.

Now you are probably saying but you do not understand the realities under which individuals, families, businesses or any organization operate today. You say to me that every business leader must be ready to set and achieve the goals and objectives of its shareholders, its boards of directors or the business will get someone else to do it. You say every parent must prepare their children to set and achieve goals for their futures and; and that every relationship should have some type goals for where that relationship is to go.

We do not disagree with these realities. We understand the market realities do not wait for the business to get itself in position to capitalize on market opportunities. You have to strike when the pitch is thrown. Where uncommon leaders differ is in when and how they prepare. *Common view leaders settle for simply setting goals because they prepare for what they think they can do; uncommon leaders are natural planners because they prepare to perform what they cannot yet do.*

Let me illustrate the importance of planning done right and goal setting done wrong. In 1999, I was asked by a very senior Pentagon Official to research and publish a white paper that would enable senior military and department of defense civilian leaders to envision the Army as it might be in the year 2025. Yes a full 25 years into the future from the time I started my research! That document, called The Army After Next (AAN) was published and it has been used by our military departments to help guide their day to day operations today.

From that document the Army could envision the need for a lighter more mobile force, so in recent years our military smartly reduced the amount of heavy equipment that was core to a Vietnam era Army. We added more individual soldiers equipped with a greater assortment and range of personal weaponry needed for the close up type of conflict we envisioned in the next years following 1999. Without a clear sense of the future possibilities and the challenges ahead for our country, the Army, like most of us as individuals and many businesses today, would have been forced to react to a need to change rather than leading a need to change.

Without a plan Army leaders would have been forced to make the best possible decisions based on circumstances as they developed. Not many businesses are in a life and death environment like our Army, but planning is no less important to the life and prosperity of a business as it is with the success of our Army in its mission to protect and defend the interests of the US and its people. Developing the organization and setting clear direction is one of the three leadership imperatives the uncommon leader follows as a matter of principle. It starts with:

Planning: Uncommon leaders get planning right! Planning is a state where the present circumstances of an individual or business or any other organization are driven from a future perspective rather than simply being an extrapolation of the past. The uncommon leader plans the future rather than plan for the future; they don't budget they invest.

In our planning programs we constantly challenge businesses and individuals to look beyond their immediate needs and desires to what is required to sustain them over the long haul. We have learned from working with uncommon people that every successful business learns to decompose its business issues; synthesize that data; and then develop plans to execute relevant business solutions.

Planning should be a process or continuous method for moving forward that will enable individuals and businesses to identify, promote and to preserve what is of distinctive value to people or to customers. Planning ahead of setting goals or before responding to problems enables the uncommon leaders to:

- Focus on transforming the business and or it's people by driving change more than reacting to change;
- Helps to provide meaning and purpose to the business, its people and especially to business customers;
- Describes in vivid terms where the business is going (direction) more than how it is growing (metrics and measures);
- Focuses the business precisely on what it is fully able to do and fully committed to executing;
- Identifies, promotes and preserves what is distinctive about individuals and the organization and;
- It is a fundamental naturally occurring element of the business.

Planning is necessary to help you and the businesses you lead to understand who you are or who your business is and what you can do to achieve or to become more. It is not goal setting as most people have come to express it. Planning benefits:

- Decision making: Make more, better and faster business and individual decisions;
- Problem solving: Understanding problems in the context of the core focus and objectives of the business or your life;
- Severity: Help reduce or minimize failures and the impact of failures;
- Recovery: Help reduce the time it takes to recover from failures;
- Impact: Help increase the scope and duration of your successes;
- Skill integration: Helps to incorporate the skills and talents of each person more effectively and;
- Transformational: Prepares you and or your business to live in a constant state of transformation.

Zion asked Confucius "what would you say if all the people of a village like a person?" "That is not enough," replied Confucius. "What would you say if all the people of the village dislike a person?" "That is not enough," replied Confucius. "It is better when the good people of the village like him and the bad people do not like him".

This ancient piece of wisdom summarizes what we want you to know and to remember about planning. Planning helps you to focus on or to become the thing that you can be best at becoming or doing. Uncommon leaders know good people and good customers and good partners are more likely to buy into your business when your plans are perceived to be good for them. They are not likely to buy into you when your goals are growth and self-focused. *Uncommon leaders have the courage to create and execute a plan to develop the self and the business to be the good that good people of our society align with and buy into.*

I have conducted planning sessions for businesses of all sizes and in all markets; and for individuals who want to change the course of their lives, personally and professionally; and for governments from local levels right on up through our national government and the governments of countries abroad. I have not found evidence of any customer of any business client who is inspired by a business goal or objective to increase revenue. Life doesn't work that way.

Make sure you take the time to plan so that you attract the right people to like you. Those that like you will commit to you and become loyal to you. Some others will not – that is just how these things work.

If you cannot share your goals with your closest clients or vendors perhaps your goal is not one that is of the best interest to you.

Developing a Playbook Mindset!

"So the abundance will be unknown in the land because of that subsequent famine; for it will be very severe".
Genesis 41:30-31

In this Bible Scripture, God tells the people of the land they will enjoy a seven year period of much prosperity followed by a seven year period of famine all across the land. During the seven years of prosperity the people developed a plan (not a goal) to take up a portion of the seven years of prosperity to be set aside to carry the people through the seven years of famine. One man was identified and set over the entire plan to ensure it was accomplished. Their lives depended on developing and executing a plan that would work. They could not risk wasting the seven years of bounty before developing a plan for the seven years of famine.

Unfortunately many businesses do not operate by this wisdom. The road is straight but they are so short termed focused that they do not accurately see far enough ahead to the period of slow or no growth that will surely follow a period of economic prosperity. They routinely allow periods of slow or no growth to develop in their business or in their markets before they awake to the need to take action.

Then during periods of famine they usually set goals that emphasize growth and prosperity rather than preparation, maintaining, enhancing and developing capabilities for the feast to come. I am reminded of something said by the CEO of a billion dollar outsourcing firm I once worked for. During a period of very tough economic times where growth was almost impossible to sustain, he said *our business should be good enough to win our share of the slow growth available within the market.*

While that is a reasonable statement and business observation, it served to set the overall focus of the business on the wrong path. People focused too much on winning business in a slow growth economy and neglected to enhance the business to be ready to sprint forward when the economy turned. Well this company survived a few years after that time – until it was sold to one of its competitors. The business could never generate the business success and momentum needed to satisfy its' desires for growth. Its goals were never in line with the natural seasons of prosperity and famine. Its' unfortunate there wasn't an uncommon leader on the team of that organization who climbed a tree and yelled down to the others *we are in the wrong mode!*

When it comes to planning business success, the uncommon leaders typically see what other leaders miss and they miss what tends to cause others to falter.

It is difficult for the good leader to always balance plans with changing priorities and the realities of things not happening according to plan. Here is some common sense often overlooked. Things will never go according to plan when you have no plan. Hoping that things will work to your benefit is not planning, it's hoping. Before hope, the uncommon leader develops purpose and adds the vision to see problems and their solutions before they happen. With vision, the uncommon leader adds the plan of action to see the vision come to life. With the plan of action, the uncommon leader is able to take the journey with the confidence of having seen the journey completed before it was started. They seem prepared for almost any event because in their vision and through their planning they have allowed themselves to experience things in their thoughts before an event happens in reality.

Purpose

All that we said regarding to planning starts with purpose. Purpose is the ultimate inner focus and life of an individual or a business. I used the word inner focus to make a clear distinction with purpose. It is not what people see that is your focus of purpose but it is what you see from within and what drives you and your business – that is your purpose. It is the reason for being and the reason behind all that individuals or a business does or intends to do.

Purpose will answer the question *what on earth are we in this business for?* Purpose itself is not a goal or task or your mission. And though you may have a goal designed to help you live your purpose, your purpose exists because you exist; it lives because you live; it is there because your business is there.

Your purpose is what you know yourself to be driven from within to be. When you follow your purpose things fall naturally into place for you; but when you try to live contrary to your purpose, life is a struggle. Without purpose success is harder to achieve and to sustain and you may never realize the pleasure of true fulfillment in life.

It is the role of the leader to help others find purpose for themselves and to help business to establish purpose for itself. The power of purpose and its impact on individual and business success is incredible. When we understand our fundamental reason for existence we are able to connect with our strengths and capabilities that are natural to us. We are able to thrive in areas where others fail because we seem to fit naturally in a particular area. When businesses take the time to discover a fundamental purpose it is able to transcend the need and goal of simply making money.

Every person has a place in their lives that waits to be filled by the discovery of real purpose. Leaders who help people reach within to discover their real purpose help make people of more value to themselves and to their businesses. Every business has a place in its existence that defines its real value to the customer; its real differentiation within the market and its real impact in society. Purpose is what does this.

Uncommon leaders watch for the signs of people who are driven by purpose. You have seen them. They are very deliberate; they make great decisions even in the face of uncertainty; they seem to be experienced and mature beyond their years; they are easily liked; they manage relationships well; they know themselves well and they seem to know you better than you know yourself; they are not easily distracted from what is important; they understand why things work; they start to rise to the top of the barrel long before the barrel is full and before they have even seen the problem they often have the solution. Uncommon leaders have the ability to recognize people like this and to help them bring the impact of their natural but untapped value to the business.

Vision

"Where there is no vision, the people cast off restraint, but happy is he that keeps the law".
Proverb

If we asked 20 people to list five characteristics of a great leader, being a visionary would undoubtedly be one of those five. Most people are smart enough to realize vision is important. They just don't know why or how it's important. The proverb we quoted always causes people to stop and ponder what does this really mean? They say within themselves we are building a business; that is our vision. Is there anything more obvious than that? Well maybe nothing. But what is wrong is the use of the idea of vision. Vision is how we visualize the end so that what we do is done with more precision, meaning and commitment.

Without vision people start and fail more than they start and succeed.

You see, said another way this proverb might provide more clarity. Where people have not envisioned within them what the future possibilities are for them, they ultimately work at so many things over time that in the end things do not come together to make them any better off.

I'm sure you know someone like this. They have always wanted to be a pilot but because they did not start by envisioning how their life as a pilot might unfold they work at lots jobs doing many things none of which moved them toward becoming the pilot they thought they could be.

Why does this happen with people; why does it happen with businesses? Well because people and business tend to develop and to work toward the urgency of the here and now more than tomorrow; we live and work to gratify desires more than we do to fulfill dreams. Where we give our lives to fulfilling our purpose; vision is to people and to business the focus of all they do. Lose sight of your vision or having no vision and you run the risk of casting off any restraint you may have had in keeping true to what your future could hold for you.

Vision is the place and or the state in the future where you or your business can see itself arriving. It is the expression of future possibilities. The uncommon leader learns to use vision to inspire people. As they develop the strength of their organizations the uncommon leader uses generous portions of vision to help remind everyone of where they are headed.

Lofty goals appeal to the mind of people but they are never sufficient to inspire and motivate people. Ultimately motivation has to come to the heart. Uncommon leaders know that people respond to vision with the heart; people are more likely to successfully act out the things they are able to envision within them. They realize that everyone should understand the organizational vision and strategic objectives so employees can see the big picture. They realize that people want to know where the organization is going and how that direction affects their personal objectives.

Vision is a vivid and compelling description or view of the possibilities that exist in your future. Maxwell refers to vision as the indispensable quality of leadership. *Vision enables people to see farther than before; to see more than before; and to see things faster than before.* It is the only thing that ensures each person is aimed in the same direction as the organization. Vision simply puts everyone on track and it keeps everyone on track.

Pearl S. Buck wrote in the book "What America Means to Me", that every great mistake has a halfway moment, a split second when it can be recalled and perhaps remedied. Uncommon leaders use vision to help see this halfway moment and to react to it with confidence and success. Without the vision to see beyond where you are today, halfway moments become the defining moments of failure for many leaders and their businesses.

Here are some examples of powerful visions by some leading businesses:

- Become the company most known for changing the worldwide poor-quality image of Japanese products" **Sony (Early 1950's)**;
- To democratize the automobile – **Ford (Early 1900's)**
- To revolutionize this company to have the speed and agility of a small enterprise – **GE**
- Powered by innovation, guided by integrity, we help our customers achieve their most challenging goals– **Lockheed Martin**;
- To give ordinary folk the chance to buy the same things as rich people – **Wal-Mart**;

- To make technical contributions for the advancement and welfare of humanity - **Hewlett-Packard.**

Let me share a little more about Sony Corporation. They have developed a creed to further express their vision. It says:

Sony – We help Dreamers Dream!

Sony is a company devoted to the celebration of life. We create things for every kind of imagination; products that stimulate the senses and refresh the spirit; ideas that always surprise and never disappoint; innovations that are easy to love and effortless to use things that are not essential yet hard to live without. We are not here to be logical or predictable. We're here to pursue infinite possibilities. We allow the brightest minds to interact freely so the unexpected can emerge. We invite new thinking so even more fantastic ideas can evolve. Creativity is our essence. We take chances. We exceed expectations. We help dreamers dream!

Sony got its start in the late 1940's and it continues today. Much of the reason it has become an enduring business can be traced to how its earliest leaders used vision to build a strong business and not just to launch a neat product. It seems they were able to overcome obstacles and hurdles that overcame lessor businesses. They do indeed h*elp dreamers dream!*

So a final thought on vision. We don't offer the insight on vision to make you a visionary. Our planning program is designed to make our leaders more effective at creating and casting vision. Our purpose with vision is to help you learn to build strong organizations; to help you transition from the natural tendency to run things to building things. In developing their organizations the uncommon leader uses the power of vision to:

- Unite the hearts of people – people learn to think together; dream together and act together;
- Give life to Purpose – people learn to live and to fulfill a shared purpose for being;
- Intensify the ability of people to recognize common ways to do more and to see uncommon ways to be more;
- Encourage innovation and creativity;
- Develop sound decision making skills;
- Develop the courage act in a timely manner;
- Enhance effective communication abilities;
- Help people learn to see beyond where they saw before;
- Help people learn to see before they saw before;
- Help people see more than they saw before and;
- Help people see what they didn't see before.

Purpose and Vision work together to become the foundations in developing strong consistent organizational and individual competencies. The illustration below will help you to visualize the impact Purpose and Vision can have in your personal life and in your business.

The Impact of Purpose and Vision

Purpose	Vision
Our reason for being – Lives and businesses are given to fulfill our purpose	The focus of our lives / businesses and all that we do
Reminds us of how we are put together	Show us how our lives / business will unfold
Reminds us of why we live and operate each day	Inspires how we live and operate each day
Confirms how we want to start our lives / businesses	A view of how we want our lives / businesses to develop
Helps us focus within to find meaning for what we CAN do	Helps us focus without to reach for the things we CANNOT do yet
Helps us see where we do not fit	Helps us see where we belong
Helps build strong organizations of people	Helps inspire commitment among an organization of strong people
Helps identify those who are alike	Helps unite those alike at their hearts

Values and Guiding Principles

"Always do what is right. It will gratify half of mankind and astound the other". Mark Twain

What Matters Most

The CEO of a billion dollar business complained to me: *We just received the results from our employee and customer survey. It seems our employees don't really trust us and our customers don't really like us. Employees say we are selfish and stingy and our customers say we provide shoddy products and service but since we are the only business in town we can get away with it inferior products and bad service.*

He lamented. *We give our employees a job and we pay them and this is the gratitude we get.* And of his customers he said *don't they understand how hard it is to build a strong successful business for our shareholders while at the same time attend to every little complaint the customer has. We cannot work the same for the customer and as we do for our shareholders. We give our customers all that we can in light of the need to give back to those who give us the most.*

This CEO was clearly confused. *Giving the most to the business doesn't make you matter the most to the customer.* So I asked him to reflect on what mattered the most to the business. Later we assembled his senior leadership team together for a half day offsite discussion of what matters most. To their surprise they were not in alignment with what was most important to the business. Some saw the bottom line as the most important; others the employees; several saw product and service quality but overall there was general misalignment with what was of core importance to the business.

What we found was simple. The values they held as individuals were very different as were the things they valued. And each leader followed their own set of guiding principles – foundations that set the boundaries for how they would operate within the business. Over the course of our half day session the leadership team realized that of all the things that mattered to them they had failed to deliver on what mattered most – creating satisfied customers.

They should have done well all the things they thought mattered and not overlooked the fundamental thing that mattered most. At the end of this section I will share the process we used with leadership team to identify the values, things valued and guiding principles that were common across each person on the team.

This problem highlights the area of leadership where the uncommon leader brings the greatest significance – identifying, creating and demonstrating a personal and professional environment of moral and ethical values. Many businesses have failed because the leader lost sight of or demonstrated an unhealthy personal and professional set of values and guiding principles.

From 1985, at its start to 2000, Enron Corporation enjoyed a status as one of the worlds' most innovative and successful companies. But just a year later, in December 2001, Enron

Corporation filed for bankruptcy and of course the company later failed. It didn't fail because of a tough market economy, though the economy did hit a recession around this time; it didn't fail because of sloppy board oversight, though that was a problem; and it didn't fail because of imaginative accounting and off-balance sheet financing though those were problems too.

Enron failed because leaders with questionable integrity made decisions of questionable ethics based questionable values and moral foundations. A quote by former President of the United States Dwight Eisenhower captures the essence of the value of values and understanding what matters most. He said, *A people that value its privileges above its principles soon lose both.*

We could assume what mattered most to Enron's leaders was achieving company objectives; the ends they desired justified whatever means they took. Whatever their motives, Enron's leaders as have many other leaders, got off track or rather took a path that led their companies, themselves and many others to personal and professional failure.

Uncommon leaders never stop trying to be the ethical and moral example for others. They know that an organization of questionable values is an organization that is perched on a slippery slope fighting two battles. The first is to overcome failure by becoming more successful than its competitors and second to win the battle it fights from within to survive leaders and people who will use most any means to justify the ends they seek for personal and professional success.

Uncommon leaders know that if you cannot win the second battle you will invariably lose the first. They also understand the battle to live your values is a highly personal thing that must be won inside the person so they devote themselves to visibly fighting their own personal and professional battle to live and operate by values of the highest degree and of unquestioned moral integrity.

Every person and every business must take the time to determine three things that form their moral and ethical foundations. They must determine for themselves the values they hold; the things they value and the principles by which they will operate.

- Values: These are deeply held beliefs about what is good, right and appropriate. They are deep-seated and remain constant over time. People accumulate values from childhood based on how they are taught, what they observe and how they are influenced. Values are the lasting tenants of an organization or of a person. They represent the enduring character and or the identity of the organization. They are the inherent sense of right and wrong; fair and unfair; they are the standards by which all actions are sifted. Following this description honesty would be a personal or professional value;

- Things we Value: These are the things that are important to us beyond the values we hold. Things we value are learned from personal tastes and desires for our lives. They are the places of emphasis in life where we assign the greatest importance to us individually. Rather than being a sense of right and wrong the things we value become our sense of good and best. Things such as friendships, leisure time, good food and so forth are examples of things we come to value;

- Guiding Principles: These are the specific set of behaviors, rules or conditions for which all actions must follow. They are the expression of what rules of operation will guide your personal and professional behavior. Guiding principles provide direction to the business in the pursuit of its purpose, vision and mission; they facilitate consistent decision making and focus on top priorities. Things such as keeping others informed, doing what is right and personal and professional accountability are a few useful guiding principles.

The United States Army has identified 11 leadership principles that are designed to guide and facilitate effective behavior and performance among its leaders. They are expressed in the paragraph below. See if you can identify the eleven principles of leadership.

Army Leadership Principles

Each leader must be tactically and technically proficient; knowing the self and seeking self-improvement in areas where development is needed. You must know your soldiers and look out for their welfare. Always keep your soldiers informed; set the right example. Ensure all tasks are understood, supervised and accomplished; train your soldiers as a team. Make sound and timely decisions and always develop a sense of responsibility in your subordinates. In the end you must employ your unit in accordance with its capabilities. Always seek additional responsibility and take responsibility for your actions.

Here are the guiding principles:

- Be tactically and technically proficient – your qualification as a leader matters;
- Know yourself and seek self-improvement – know and reject your own short comings;
- Know your soldiers and look out for their welfare – know and take care of your soldiers needs always;
- Keep soldiers informed – soldiers should never have to guess or wonder about what is going on;
- Be the right example – soldiers will follow your actions, make them right;
- Ensure tasks are understood; explain why as much as you explain what and how;

- Train soldiers as a team – it takes training as a team to become a team;
- Make sound timely decision; keep the big picture in mind to guide your decision making;
- Develop a sense of responsibility – first personally then in your soldiers;
- Employ your unit properly – use them in the way they are trained to be used;
- Seek responsibility and take responsibility for your actions; there is always more to be done than what someone is responsible to do.

Leaders of uncommon effectiveness use guiding principles to remind others of how they should think; to guide others in how they should act and to prepare others for the challenges of developing a strong successful organization.

Values / Things Valued / Guiding Principles

Attribute	Description	Use
Values	Deeply held beliefs; the inner self	The source of thoughts and the basis for our actions
Things Valued	Desired things that are priority important to us – external	Serves to explain the motivation of our actions
Guiding Principles	The accountable standards for how we behave	Creates uncommon synergies among people and organizations by guiding all actions

| Footprints | Chapter Ten | Behavior Guidelines |

Discovering Values Process

Leaders discover values, things valued and guiding principles by following a simple but effective process. See if you can match the value to the business in the table below by drawing a line to connect one to the other.

Business Values Matrix

Value	Business
Creativity and Innovation	Nordstrom's
Imagination	Procter & Gamble
Product Excellence	Sony
Service to the Customer	Disney

See next page for the correct alignment.

You can use this little drill to stress that values not lived are probably not values at all. Each of these businesses is known by its action to express a particular value. Another well-known business, Yahoo, has the following core values: Excellence, Innovation; Customer Fixation; Teamwork; Community and; Fun. You don't have to know much about Yahoo to know that these core values seem to be very appropriate for what you do know about that business.

So how did Yahoo create a set of core values that expresses the very nature of their business? Well they examined themselves in truth to express what they found within or what they genuinely wanted to act out in everyday behavior.

Leaders must ultimately model the things they say. We are all often guilty of judging ourselves by the intents of our hearts but we judge others by the harsher reality of their actions. For leadership to be effective we must learn to align our intents to our actions. In business we must learn to align the actions of our leaders to the intents and promises the business makes in the market place.

Business Values Matrix

Value	Business
Creativity and Innovation	Sony
Imagination	Disney
Product Excellence	Product Excellence
Service to the Customer	Nordstrom's

An environment where these things are misaligned will have an adverse impact on people of the business and ultimately on the perspective the customer has toward the business leaders. With Footprints we show you how to strengthen your leadership by working hard to translate what you stand for in intents to a set of leadership behaviors the effective leader must embody.

This table illustrates what we mean and the importance of clear alignment between things intended and things done:

	The organization is known for…	Leaders at this organization are known for…
Wal-Mart	Always low prices	Managing costs efficiently, getting things done on time
FedEx	Absolutely, positively, doing whatever it takes	Managing logistics, meeting deadlines, solving problems quickly
Lexus	Pursuit of perfection	Managing quality processes for continuous improvements
Procter & Gamble	Brands you know and trust	Developing consumer insights, precisely targeted marketing, product innovation
McKinsey	Being a CEO's trusted partner	Leading teams that deconstruct problems, synthesize data, and develop solutions
Boeing	People working as a global enterprise for aerospace leadership	Solving global problems, working as teams, possessing technical excellence in aerospace
Apple	Innovation and design	Creating new products and services that break industry norms
PepsiCo	Appealing to the younger generation	Building the next generation of talent
Your Company	?	?

Harvard Business Review – 2007

You can start the process of discovering your values or the values for your business by assembling a list of values from among your leaders and others in the company. Always start by considering the Purpose, Vision and Mission of the business. Here is a list of values you can use to practice this process:

Integrity: Adhering to moral and ethical principles; sound character; honesty and trustworthiness

Character: Having moral and ethical foundation of honesty, courage and integrity

Honesty: Adhering to operating on a basis of truth; the trait of being truthful, upright and fair

Loyalty: Giving commitment and full obligation and adherence to a person or thing

Respect: Acknowledging the worth, value and excellence of a person or persons

Empathy: Identifying with the experiences, feelings, and thoughts of another

Courage: Facing a difficulty, danger and or adversity without fear but with bravery and determination

Wisdom: Appropriately discerning facts and knowledge; acting and responding appropriately with uncommon insight

Generosity: Freely and gladly giving of oneself or of an organization things value

Quality: Adhering to the highest standards of excellence; producing things that are free of defects

Step1 – Have each person privately reduce this list by half by eliminating the five items that are of the least importance to them. Make sure your mind is set to eliminate those five that are least important to you at this point. You are not keeping those that are more important – that will come in a later step.

Step 2 – Now have each person reduce the remaining list again by half or down to three remaining items. Again they are to eliminate those items that are of least importance to them.

Step 3 – Once again eliminate least important items until you have only two items remaining.

Step 4 – Now choose from the remaining two or three items the two values that are most important to you.

You can then have each person compare results. But following this process or a similar process will allow each person to make independent unbiased choices about what is inherently more important to them. You are then able to start your discussion of what is or should be important to the business and determine the value set that will work for the business and for the people.

The Stages of Uncommon Development

Footprints is an examination of the journey uncommon leaders take to become uncommonly great leaders. It is a look at what matters most in all the things that matter at all. There are five discrete steps along this journey. Each step challenges the leader to make changes within the leader that drives the uncommon actions we see. When a person understands what happens within or what should happen within it is more likely he will make the inner transformation needed to produce lasting and more powerful outward actions.

Uncommon leaders seemingly always lead by explaining why so we use this approach in explaining the stages of development. With each stage we explore why this stage is important to the results we desire. As much as possible we also follow the learning to teaching model we explained earlier – tell them the steps only and the will likely forget; show them the steps and they will likely remember; but involve them in the steps and they can possibly learn. The steps of uncommon development are:

- The Footprints of Maturation! First learning to be successful with you.
    - Why is it important? Because this is where the seeds of trust and respect are sown.

- The Footprints of Qualification! Becoming unquestionably qualified and competent.
    - Why is it important? Because this is where the seeds of vision, purpose and alignment with and confidence in the leader are sown.
- The Footprints of Collaboration! Learning to connect with others.
    - Why is it important? Because this is where the seeds of influence and respect are sown.
- The Footprints of Determination! Learning how to be successful and to get things done through the efforts of others.
    - Why is this important? Because this is where the seeds of commitment, loyalty and belief in the leader are sown.
- The Footprints of Transformation! Learning to develop leaders more than followers.
    - Why is this important! Because this is where the seeds of identification and authenticity are sown.

Footprints of Maturation is the foundation for leading the self well; fail to master your maturation as a leader and people will not trust you.

Footprints of Qualification is the foundation for uncommon positional success; fail to master your qualifications as a leader and people will not believe in you.

Footprints of Collaboration is the foundation for relational leadership success; fail to master the ability to connect with and collaborate with people and they will not be influenced by you.

Footprints of Determination is the foundation for achieving successful results; fail to learn to produce through the efforts of others and they will not commit to you.

Footprints of Transformation is the foundation for successfully developing leaders more than followers; fail to personify an effective leader and to master the ability to transform others and they will not resonate with or recognize you as a leader.

Footprints of Maturation

"The greatest indication of a mature person is the one who pays attention to the things that are critical to the people who are critical in his life"
Footprints

A professor standing before his Philosophy class had some items in front of him. When class began he picked up a very large empty mayonnaise jar and proceeded to fill it with golf balls. He then asked the students if the jar was full. They agreed that it was. The professor then picked up a box of pebbles and poured them into the jar. He shook the jar lightly. The pebbles rolled into the open areas between the golf balls. He then asked the students again if the jar was full. They agreed it was. The professor next picked up a box of sand and poured it into the jar. Of course the sand filled up everything else. He asked once again if the jar was full. The students responded with a unanimous yes.

The professor then produced two cups of coffee from under the table and poured the entire contents into the jar effectively filling the empty spaced between the sand. The students laughed.

Now the professor said, as the laughter subsided, *I want you to recognize that this jar represents your life. The golf balls are the important things in your life – God, family, your children, your health, your friends and your favorite passions – things that if everything else was lost and only they remained, your life would still be full.*

The pebbles are the other things that matter to you but not as important as your golf balls; things like your job, your house and your car. The Sand is everything else – the small stuff. If you put the sand into the jar first he continued, there is no room for the pebbles or the golf balls.

The same goes for life. If you spend all your time and energy on the small stuff you will never have room for the things that are really important in life. *Pay attention to the things that are critical to the people who are critical in your life.*

Your maturity; your attitude, your health, your perspective these are all things about you that are crucial to others and the quality of life they can enjoy with you. Learn to be a successful spouse; play with and grow with your children; take time to spend with family and friends; take care of your health; play a round of golf; become great at your work; keep your priorities straight. Take care of the big important things and keep them in perspective. Everything else is just sand. If you do this, no matter how full your life may seem, there will always seem to be room for a little more sand. *Always make certain your maturity is greater than your age; people are watching how you have grown up.*

Maturation Stage of Leadership Development (BE)

It's about! Self-maturation!

- Self-awareness - how effective you are at leading others depends on where you are willing to start working on yourself;
- Self-assurance - it is about developing a positive attitude and about recognizing and overcoming personal weaknesses;
- Self-control - it is about developing a respected overall perspective rather than a questionable perspective.

Leader focus:

- Development – learning to develop sound personal and professional foundations for life;
- Attitude – learning to see the upside in things when the downside is what others see.

Leader effectiveness depends on:

- Self-transformation – learning to change others, your surroundings and your impact by transforming who you are;
- Humility - your attitude toward learning to follow and learning to operate effectively under the authority of others;
- Response to Challenges – developing courage, conviction and integrity; learning to grow from challenges rather than to be overcome by challenges;
- Understanding human nature – knowing who you are and taking steps to become better tomorrow than you are today – rejecting your own marginal attributes.

How people respond to you:
- The more mature you are the more mature others act;
- They give or withhold trust based on how they feel about your maturity;
- The more they trust you the more they will act with trust toward you.

Progression as a leader depends on:
- Standing out! The contributions you make when you are not the leader;
- Standing for! The contributions you make toward others;
- Standing apart! The contributions you make beyond what is expected.

Uncommon leaders never under estimate the importance of maturity. They understand the person who has learned to be faithful in developing the little things in themselves that are vital to leading themselves well – these people will be faithful in how they handle the bigger things required to develop others to achieve their own success. I heard a story about a new CEO. This story is a great summary of what it means and the benefit of maturing and not just getting older.

Chapter Twelve

The New CEO

A successful business man was growing old and knew it was time to choose a successor to take over the business. Instead of choosing one of his directors or his children he decided to do something different. He called all the young executives in his company together. He said, *it is time for me to step down and choose the next CEO.*

I have decided to choose one of you. The young executives were shocked, but the boss continued. *I am going to give each one of you a SEED today - one very special SEED. I want you to plant the seed, water it, and come back here one year from today with what you have grown from the seed I have given you. I will then judge the plants that you bring, and the one I choose, that owner will be the next CEO.*

One man, named Jim, was there that day and he, like the others, received a seed. He went home and excitedly, told his wife the story. She helped him get a pot, soil and compost and he planted the seed. Every day he would water it and watch to see if it had grown. After about three weeks, some of the other executives began to talk about their seeds and the plants that were beginning to grow. Jim kept checking his seed, but nothing ever grew. Three weeks, four weeks, five weeks went by, still nothing.

By now, others were talking about their plants, but Jim didn't have a plant and he felt like a failure. Six months went by -- still nothing in Jim's pot. He just knew he had killed his seed. Everyone else had trees and tall plants, but he had nothing. Jim didn't say anything to his colleagues. However, he just kept watering and fertilizing the soil - He so wanted the seed to grow.

A year finally went by and all the young executives of the company brought their plants to the CEO for inspection. Jim told his wife that he wasn't going to take an empty pot. But she asked him to be honest about what happened. Jim felt sick to his stomach; it was going to be the most embarrassing moment of his life, but he knew his wife was right. He took his empty pot to the board room.

When Jim arrived, he was amazed at the variety of plants grown by the other executives. They were beautiful -- in all shapes and sizes. Jim put his empty pot on the floor and many of his colleagues laughed, a few felt sorry for him!

When the CEO arrived, he surveyed the room and greeted his young executives. Jim just tried to hide in the back. *My what great plants, trees and flowers you have grown* said the CEO. *Today one of you will be appointed the next CEO!* All of a sudden, the CEO spotted Jim at the back of the room with his empty pot. He ordered the Financial Director to bring him to the front.

Jim was terrified. He thought, *The CEO knows I'm a failure! Maybe he will have me fired.* When Jim got to the front, the CEO asked him what had happened to his seed - Jim told him the story. The CEO asked everyone to sit down except Jim. He looked at Jim, and then announced to the young executives, *Behold your next Chief Executive Officer! His name is Jim!* Jim couldn't believe it. Jim couldn't even grow his seed. *How could he be the new CEO?* The others said.

Then the CEO said, *One year ago today, I gave everyone in this room a seed. I told you to take the seed, plant it, water it, and bring it back to me today. But I gave you all boiled seeds; they were dead - it was not possible for them to grow. All of you, except Jim, have brought me trees and plants and flowers. When you found that the seed would not grow, you substituted another seed for the one I gave you. Jim was the only one with the maturity, courage and honesty to bring me a pot with my seed in it. Therefore, he is the one who will be the new Chief Executive Officer!* The CEO told them that Jim planted honesty so he reaped trust; he planted goodness so the CEO became his friend; he planted humility so he stood in greatness; he planted perseverance so he was the only one satisfied; he planted hard work so he reaped the success of being named the next CEO; and he planted maturity so he was able to do what none of the others could do.

What you mature to be in life; life ultimately gives back to you. *The uncommon leader is always uncommonly more mature than it seems to be for the common leader.*

| Footprints | Chapter Thirteen | Earning Their Belief |

Footprints of Qualification

"There is nothing which rots morale more quickly and more completely than the feeling that those in authority do not know their own minds." Lionel Urwick, Harvard Business Review 1956

Top Leaders

A woman in a hot air balloon realized she was lost. She reduced altitude and spotted a man below. She descended a bit more and shouted, *Excuse me Sir, can you help me? I promised a friend I would meet him an hour ago but I don't know where I am.* The man below replied, *you are in a hot air balloon hovering approximately 30 feet above the ground. You're between 40 and 41 degrees north latitude and between 59 and 60 degrees west longitude.*

You must be an engineer, said the lady balloonist. *I am,* replied the man. *How did you know? Well,* answered the lady in the balloon, *everything you told me is technically correct, but I have no idea what to make of your information and the fact is I'm still lost. Frankly, you've not been much help to me at all. If anything, you've delayed my trip even more.*

The engineer below responded *you must be in leadership. I am,* replied the lady balloonist, *but, how did you know? Well,* said the Engineer, *You don't know where you are or where you're going.*

You made a promise which you've no idea how to keep and you expect people beneath you to solve your problems.

The Qualification Stage of Development (KNOW)

Uncommon leaders understand they do not have to know everything but they should know what they ought to know. A leader must have a certain level of knowledge to be qualified and competent. Qualification is more than just background or previous work experiences. The uncommon leader must acquire knowledge and develop the aptitude to effectively demonstrate that knowledge across four domains crucial to leader success and the success of others. Leaders must develop effective interpersonal skills, knowledge of people and the ability to work with them.

They must have conceptual skills sufficient to enable them to understand and apply the functional and technical skills and other ideas required to do a job well. They must master the day to day qualifications to make the right decisions concerning what is best for the people and the businesses they lead. Day to day qualifications include mastery of skills appropriate to the leader's level of responsibility and accountability and they are amplified by the other skills -- interpersonal, conceptual, and technical.

But the uncommon leader is not satisfied with just knowing how to do what will get the organization through today; they are also concerned about what it will need tomorrow. The uncommon leader always strives to master the job they have and to be ready for the next job they are required to do.

Uncommon leaders are different from good leaders in that they add to their qualifications, knowledge and skills every day; they always seek out opportunities and look for ways to always increase their professional qualifications. At the qualification stage of effectiveness they are focused on always ensuring they are qualified for the roles they must perform. Anything short of that would be a personal failure to them. Qualification is shifting the focus of things from what the role requires to what the leader demonstrates.

Qualification Stage of Leadership Development (KNOW)

It's about! Competence! In the words of Darwin Smith, former CEO of Kimberly-Clark, *you should never stop trying to become qualified for your job.* It is about developing unquestioned competence around all that you need to know as a leader. It is about establishing your qualifications to be a leader beyond or apart from what the role requires. The uncommon leader does not respond to a job announcement by matching job requirements for the position against the resume of experiences and background the leader has gained.

The uncommon leader stands out for qualifications that stand out. When a position requires someone to lead others the uncommon leader stands out not just as a leader but as a developer of other leaders.

Leader focus:
- Transactional – At the qualification stage of leadership development the focus of the leader is primarily on accomplishing tasks;
- Positional – The leader performs to the level expected and required for the position.

Leader effectiveness depends on:
- Transactional / task focused – using people to accomplish tasks;
- Authority derived – effectiveness is limited to the authority the leader has within the position;
- Position restrained – people perform only to the level of their job descriptions or to what the leader instructs them to do;
- Mind driven – leaders connect more with their heads than with their hearts and people do the same.

People respond to the leader by:
- View of Leader – The leader is seen as the boss or as the one in charge not as a leader;
- Morale - Highly motivated or highly competent people are probably discouraged because they are not task focused they are transformational focused self-starting people;
- Qualification - People see the leader's abilities and qualifications as no greater than their own and;
- Connection - People connect with their minds more than with their hearts.

Progression as a leader depends on:

- Qualification – Becoming the best at something. Proving to yourself and demonstrating to others you are unquestionably qualified to excel as a leader – their leader;
- Competence – Mastering what you must know to be qualified as a leader;
- Proficiency – Learning how to use and to perfect all that you know to improve your personal and professional effectiveness and the effectiveness of others.

The qualification stage of effectiveness can be summed up this way. Uncommon leaders make it a point to study, to commit and to train relentlessly to show that they are approved before others in the roles they are asked to play for others. They make it a personal challenge to learn more about more things than they thought they could ever learn.

Footprints of Collaboration

"The single most important ingredient in the formula for success is in knowing how to get along with people". Theodore Roosevelt

A boss complained to his mentor. *My people don't like me. They say I am mean and uncaring, selfish and impossible to get along with. They don't seem to realize that in the end all I do is done to help them be successful.* The mentor said *well maybe the story of the cow and the pig has a lesson for you. The pig came to the cow and complained. People always talk about your friendliness and how much you give them. I know you are friendly and you give a lot. You give them milk. But they get much, much more from me. They get ham and bacon and lard and they even cook my feet. And yet – no one tells me they like me. To all of them I'm just a pig, a hog. Why is that? The cow thought it over a bit and then said: Perhaps it's because I give while I am still alive!*

Learn to connect with others while they live and when they are with you and when they need it. People who cannot get along with you may not be there in the end to enjoy the things you are doing for them. The interpersonal relations stage of development is the one that can bring immediate failure. With maturity and qualifications others may give you time to grow and to develop. But if you do not have the people skills to get along with others they will not give you time to learn. It is fairly common in our leadership development programs to find one or two executives in each session who believe it doesn't matter if people like them or not.

I have heard many leaders say *they don't have to like me they just need to do their jobs.* Developing great interpersonal skills doesn't mean you spend your time trying to get people to like you. But people certainly must not dislike you as the leader. We typically ask leaders taking our program to choose between the following two statements the one that best fits them personally:

- I get along with others or;
- Others get along with me.

There is no right or wrong or best response. The purpose of the question is to highlight with the leader the importance of people being able to get along with one another. People who get along will usually stay longer; they bond better; they collaborate more effectively and they support one another more. Jim Collins' says in his book "Good to Great" *those who build great companies understand the ultimate throttle on growth for any great company is not markets or technology or competition or even production. It is one thing above all others – the ability to get and to keep enough of the right people on board.*

Uncommon leaders approach the interpersonal stage of development with more focus than others; they take responsibility for making every single relationship work because each relationship is vital to their objectives.

The greatest challenge to effectively developing positive interpersonal skill is in transforming yourself. Most leaders who fail at developing strong effective interpersonal skills do so because they are more self-focused than people-focused. Connecting with others means the leader takes time to get to know others and to empathize with them; to respect them; and to become a resource for them.

A 2008 Business Week article lists 20 bad habits complied by executive coach Marshall Goldsmith describing cause leaders to fail. You can see that many of these directly relate to poor interpersonal skills:

- The need to win at all costs and in all situations—when it matters, when it doesn't and when it's totally beside the point;
- Adding Too Much Value: The overwhelming desire to add two cents to every discussion;
- Passing Judgment: The need to rate others and impose your standards on them;
- Making Destructive Comments: The needless sarcasms and cutting remarks that we think make us sound sharp and witty;
- Starting with "No," "But," or "However": The overuse of these qualifiers which secretly say to everyone, "I'm right. You're wrong";
- Telling the World How Smart We Are: The need to show people we're smarter than they think we are;

- Speaking When Angry: Using emotional volatility as a management tool;
- Negativity: The need to share our negative thoughts even when we weren't asked.
- Withholding Information: The refusal to share information in order to maintain an advantage over others;
- Failing to Give Proper Recognition: The inability to praise and reward;
- Claiming Credit We Don't Deserve: The most annoying way to overestimate our contribution to any success;
- Making Excuses: The need to reposition our annoying behavior as a permanent fixture so people excuse us for it;
- Clinging to the Past: The need to deflect blame away from ourselves and onto events and people from our past; a subset of blaming everyone else;
- Playing Favorites: Failing to see that we are treating someone unfairly;
- Refusing to Express Regret: The inability to take responsibility for our actions, admit we're wrong or recognize how our actions affect others;
- Not Listening: The most passive-aggressive form of disrespect for colleagues;
- Failing to Express Gratitude: The most basic form of bad manners;
- Punishing the Messenger: Attacking the innocent;

- Passing the Buck: The need to blame everyone but ourselves;
- An Excessive Need to Be "Me": Exalting our faults as virtues simply because they exemplify who we are.

These type behaviors are typical of people who place self-interest before anything else. These people are more task-focused than people focused. They see power, authority and status as the expression of their leadership.

Jay Hall, of the company Telemetrics, conducted a study of performance with hundreds of executives and found a direct correlation between achievement and caring and connecting with others. You can see this in the illustration below:

Achiever / Connecting Matrix

High Achiever	Average Achiever	Low Achiever
Cared about people and profit	Focused more on production	Preoccupied with own security
Respected subordinates	Focused more on own status	Showed biased distrust of subordinates
Seeks advice of subordinates	Reluctant to seek subordinate advice	Won't seek subordinate advice
Listens well to everyone	Listens only to superiors	Avoids communication and relies on policies and position
Rejects leader privileges	Embraces leader privileges	Seeks leader privileges

The military has a term "rank has its privileges". It means with the rank you achieves comes some rights and privileges you wouldn't otherwise have. Weak leaders operate with this mindset. They believe that because they are the leader it gives them the right or privilege to be a little emotional in their interpersonal relations; they can be a little impatient in their relationships; they can be a little excessive and make more judgments because they are the leader.

They believe as long as they produce, the things they achieve justify the ways they do it; production and technical skills over principles. They rationalize that some interpersonal problems will be a natural part of doing business where people are involved. It goes with the territory.

Such thinking is faulty of course but businesses have come to unwittingly or willingly allow poor leadership behaviors because of the desperate need for successful performance. Uncommon leaders hold themselves to a higher standard of behavior. Rather than look for privileges that come with the leader's territory they look within their territory for opportunities to give privileges to others.

They understand gratitude is the attitude that connects. They believe if they cannot conduct themselves in a way that others can connect with or get along with then they cannot be a leader at all.

I was once contracted by a company to deliver a development seminar for its middle level leaders; their focus was to teach leaders how to deal with difficult people. At the start of the session I asked this question. What happens if the difficult person is the leader? After some discussion we decided it would be of greater value to spend our time focused on teaching leaders how not to be difficult people.

Learning to deal with difficult people is a competence the business decided it didn't need to perfect. Weak leaders too easily accept that difficult people are a natural part of our lives or our businesses so they devise ways to work around or to control their impact; but uncommon people know that it doesn't have to be this way. Uncommon leaders change the culture in which business is conducted to expect great behavior while rejecting difficult behaviors.

Uncommon leaders know that getting along with others and being persons others can get along with are not mutually exclusive. The leader has the control to impact both, first in how they behave for themselves and then how they behave toward others. Weak leaders expect others to accept their shortcomings and leadership faults while the leader often is not prepared to accept those same faults and weaknesses in others.

You cannot effectively connect with others when you demand relationships that are one way - yours. At the collaboration stage of effectiveness people begin to distinguish the leader from any position or role of the leader. As those who are led gain confidence in the leader's interpersonal abilities they begin to identify with the leader at the level of what can be; people voluntarily begin to give the leader their permission to be led.

Chapter Fourteen — Earning Influence

Collaboration – The Path to Interpersonal Relations

It's about! Influence and the ability to connect with others! The leader learns to invest as much into the relationship with others as what is expected or taken from the relationship; to become more value to others than cost to others; to create the vision of a future that others believe in and embrace as their own; and to become a key catalyst in the success of others. *Maxwell says people will follow because of what they believe you can do for them.*

Leader focus:
- Transformational – changing the self to change others and;
- Serving – giving more than is taken.

Leader effectiveness depends on:
- From transactional to transformational;
- Dependent on connecting more with the heart of others than the mind of others;
- Dependent on an inspiring vision others buy into;
- Respecting others for the value they bring;
- Developing others to be more than they are today.

People respond to the leader by:
- Believing and trusting in the leader;
- Seeing you as their leader more than as their boss;
- Moving their commitment from their heads to heads to their hearts;

- Producing as much for you as you invest in them.

Leader progression depends on:
- Your ability to use the commitment of people to build a stronger organization;
- Your ability to establish purpose and meaning for others beyond their role;
- What you BE, KNOW and DO for others;
- Your ability to create relationships in which others find more value;
- Your ability to achieve results through others not just with others.

Poorly developed interpersonal skill is an area where weak leaders would like to take a pass. As we saw in those 20 areas that cause leaders to fail, weak leaders would prefer to make excuses for their poor behavior as a way to get others to excuse them for it. Weak leaders come to say of their behavior *it's just who I am. I'm really not bad at all – I just have a little quirk in my armor. You can overlook that and still connect with me. I'm good. I'm good.*

I heard a story about Jorge Rodriquez, a bank robber from Mexico who operated in the early 1900's along the US border with Mexico in a number of small Texas towns. He was so successful that the Texas Rangers established a special task force to try and catch him.

One afternoon one of the Rangers spotted Rodriquez as he slipped back into Mexico from Texas. The Ranger trailed him at a

Chapter Fourteen

discrete distance. When Rodriquez went into his favorite cantina to relax, the Ranger slipped in and got the drop on him. With a gun to the head of Rodriquez, the Ranger said, *Jorge Rodriquez, I know who you are. I've come to take back all the money you have stolen from Texas banks. Unless you give it to me I'm going to blow your brains out.*

Rodriquez could see the Ranger's badge and could discern his hostile intent. But there was one problem. He did not speak English. Nervously he began to speak rapidly in Spanish. But the Ranger couldn't understand him because he couldn't speak Spanish. Just then a young boy came up and spoke to the Ranger in English. *Sir, do you want me to help he asked? I can act as a translator. I speak both English and Spanish.*

The Ranger, grateful for the offer of help, respectfully asked the young boy to tell Rodriquez all the Ranger had said. The young boy turned to Rodriquez and explained that the Ranger wanted him to return the money or he would kill him. Rodriquez was insulted by the Ranger. He spoke quickly to young boy in a harsh demeaning tone telling him to tell the Ranger the money was hidden at the bottom of a well in the middle of town – all the money was there; he had not spent a cent.

He told the young boy to tell the Ranger quickly. He then insulted the young boy by calling him names and he spoke angrily about the boy's parents. He told the boy to go get some of his men or he would see to it that the young boy and his family were killed. The young boy nodded with perfect respect. He turned to the

Ranger and said *Senor Rodriquez is a brave man; he said he is ready to die today.*

A at that moment Senor Rodriquez could have used a short course in interpersonal relations. The six most important words we can ever use in our interpersonal relations: *I admit that I was wrong.* The five most important words: *You did a great job.* The four most important words: *What do you think?* The three most important words: *Could you please?* The two most important words: *Thank you.* The most important word: *We.* The least important word: *I*

Power and authority can come and go as quickly as someone can get the drop on you. Your ability to relate to others positively and to connect with them are the things that last when all else in a relationship is gone. Connecting and your interpersonal relationship skills are not the difference between life and death but success and failure depends on them.

Maya Angelou is quoted to have said *People will forget what you said. They will forget what you did. But they will never forget how you made them feel.* Uncommon leaders know they cannot afford to take a pass on developing uncommon interpersonal skills. Weak leaders may get by for a while with poor interpersonal skills because they rely on authority, power and positional status to get people to do what they want them to do.

But people will not permit themselves to be influenced by someone who does not have remarkable people skills. And just like Senor Rodriquez, power and authority over people will ultimately run its course.

I know some of you will probably say but Allen, some people will take advantage of the leader when this approach is used. Some people only care about what they can get for themselves. The leader has to have a stick to go with the carrot.

This seems like common sense to many. But uncommon leaders do common things uncommonly well. They find a deeper more effective sense about things before it becomes common to others.

Some people will try to take advantage of the leader but you don't have to permit them to do that; some people only care about themselves but you must work to change that. And as for the stick and the carrot, the uncommon leader sees success and failure differently. They use the carrot of great behavior to lead and inspire others. But they give others the stick, so that in their development they can use it to help themselves learn to be accountable, to learn to follow well and to learn to behave in ways that are expected of everyone.

Here are the principles by which uncommon people learn to develop great interpersonal skills:

- Spend time with others; you will learn helpful things you didn't know;
- Empathize with others; they will believe you care;
- Have a message about where you want to go with them; they will see where you are;
- Invest in others; they will give returns to you;
- Listen to others; they will speak freely with you;

- Take responsibility for your behaviors; it will make it easier for others to take responsibility for theirs;
- And be accountable to others; they will hold themselves accountable to you.

If you get along others will go along. Take into your relationships what you want to get from them. Have the best interests of others at heart and they will have your interest at heart. Decide to make a difference to others by becoming a significance to others. Encourage their hearts and inspire their minds. And finally, never make someone feel as if their failure is the only good you see in them.

In your interpersonal relations be careful of anyone; especially when he is someone who does not advise well. Never allow anyone to convince you that you cannot bring out the best in someone; never let someone convince you that you cannot get the most from everyone. Give everyone your best and anyone you touch will likely become someone you can count on for their best.

Without great interpersonal skills you don't have connection; without connection you don't have influence and; without influence you don't have people committed to go or to follow where you are going.

Footprints of Determination

"Nothing in the world can take the place of persistence. Talent will not; nothing is more common than unsuccessful men with great talent. Genius will not; unrewarded genius is a proverb. Education will not; the world is full of educated derelicts. Persistence and determination alone are omnipotent". Sign on the wall of Ray Kroc (1902-1984), founder of McDonald's restaurants (they are the words of Calvin Coolidge).

Achieving results is a feature of effective leadership that cannot be overlooked. No great leader would consider himself to be a successful leader if he didn't achieve results. Jim Collins in his book "Good to Great" explains the special nuance we find in his level five leaders. He says level five leaders have an unwavering resolve and an intense professional will to do what must be done. They have an almost unstoppable resolve, almost stoic determination to do whatever it takes to make people and the companies they run great.

People who've learned to get things done are different from those who simply try hard! You will know them when you see them because they stand out and they stand apart from others. Remember my conversation with Dana from one of our leadership development seminars. Dana said she became consistently more successful with others when she first learned to be successful with herself. She got it! And uncommon leaders get it! It is that sense of knowing how to get things done first through themselves and then through the efforts of others. This is what separates the uncommon leader from a good leader. Results matter! Results the leader helps others to achieve matter more! People like to be a part of a winning team!

He Gets It!

I am reminded of a 2010 news article that spoke about a guest on a TV program, The Jerry Tarkanian Show. Tarkanian is a very successful college basketball coach who now has a sports TV program. He interviews a variety of athletes and sports people on a variety of subjects.

One program focused on why some professional sports teams seem to win more consistently than others. There were a ton of reasons offered but one interview in particular shed light on the type of players who get it; they understand what winning is about. These players are different from others who have great talent and skills. The story is about the Chicago Bulls, a professional team in the National Basketball Association, NBA and its interview of the top two college players entering the NBA in 2008, Michael Beasley and Derrick Rose.

Before the NBA draft that year both Beasely and Rose had interviews with Chicago's front office personnel including owner Jerry Reinsdorf. The Bulls first met with Michael Beasley, who was coming off a banner collegiate season; based on his skills and talents he was sure to be one of the top three college basketball players selected for the NBA that year.

The story was told that during the session with Beasley and the Bulls, there were a couple occasions in which (one of) his (*two*) cell phones went off. And believe it or not, *he answered the calls!* New Bulls head coach Vinny Del Negro advised Beasley that he was meeting with *the owner* and that, at that time, there couldn't be too many things more important than listening to what Mr. Reinsdorf had to say and answering whatever questions the people at the meeting had of him.

When Reinsdorf posed the question, *What about college basketball bothered you most?* Beasley contemplated for a moment and then said w*hen you go on the road and when the referees make bad calls.*

When it was Rose's turn in front of the brass, he sat up straight and was totally focused. He had a thorough grasp of the magnitude of the encounter. He put his ego aside. Consider this is a guy who won back-to-back state titles in high school and went *38-2* in his only season in college, dropping the national championship game in overtime. What was his response to Reinsdorf's question, *What about college basketball bothered you most? Rose replied* **"Losing!"** Nothing more, simply losing. The guy hates losing and that alone is probably why he is the winner that he is today.

His answer speaks of the kind of guy Derrick Rose is and why he's destined for (even more) greatness. Rose isn't as tall as Beasley; he cannot jump as high as Beasley and at the time of the draft he probably could not shoot the ball as well as Beasley. But the Bulls made him the first player selected in the NBA draft that year. They have not been disappointed. He is perhaps the best point guard or one of the three best in the whole NBA. In 2011, he was voted the league's most valuable player. The Bulls have had a winning record in each year since Rose arrived.

When they talk about drafts picks in the NBA they discuss athleticism, outside shot, basketball IQ, college success, vertical leap and the other things coaches and fans can see and measure. But maturity, determination and passion for the game and the craft matter more in how a player develops. Competitiveness matters a lot more than jumping ability; it may seem difficult to observe and to measure and many teams seem to ignore it. But then those are probably the teams who cannot develop a consistent winning track record. Derrick Rose and players like him get it! Determination is the leader's key to learning to get things done; it's the key to learning to produce through the efforts of others. Without determination it is impossible to earn the commitment of others. Without the commitment of others leaders don't lead they pull. Uncommon leaders learn that they can inspire even the uninspired by learning and teaching others to get things done consistently.

So what is the difference between Derek Rose and Michael Beasley? What is the difference between the person who consistently produces and the one who doesn't? Why does one person have an uncommon will and drive to achieve and another does not? Well it's not talent. Uncommonly productive people are not always the most talented people. It's not intelligence.

Uncommonly productive people use their intelligence differently but they are not more intelligent than others.

How they are different is found in the determination by which they live each day. Uncommon people are more productive because through their determination they:

D	Drive themselves by purpose and develop others to do the same;
E	Excel at doing what others fail to do;
T	Transform their way of thinking from common to uncommon;
E	Execute with precision; they finish what they start;
R	Remain focused on the most important – nothing distracts them;
M	Master what they must BE KNOW and DO for their organizations;
I	Invest in making others better than they are;
N	Nothing is too small for them that it cannot be done well;
A	Accountable to themselves to be accountable for others;
T	Timely in how they make decisions;
I	Insight is uncommon; their wisdom is greater than experience;
O	Opportunities are seen where others see problems
N	Never permit fear hold them back; fear inspires an *I can do it* spirit.

So you might say this sounds very much like someone who is overly optimistic or pulled by blind optimism. Maybe so, but - leaders who are blindly optimistic are self-deceived. They promote a sunny outlook even when the facts say there is reason for caution or concern. They ignore reality and instead focus on inspiring hope that things will change for the better; good times always come around after bad times. The blindly optimistic leader sets lofty goals that appeal to our need and desire to have something great to happen for us but these goals are unattainable. But when we speak of the uncommon leader's determination we speak of the person who is not led by his own blindness to the facts but a person who takes the facts and circumstance into full consideration before setting themselves upon a path to success. When they put their hands to the plow they don't let go until they reach the end of the row; they learn from the same things that burn others; they see lessons where others see problems and they seem to have knowledge and insight before that same knowledge is available to others. Here is how the stoically determined leader is different from the overly optimistic leader:

Highly Successful / Blindly Optimistic

Stoically Determined	Blindly Optimistic
Transparency – you always know the basis of their determination – fact or fiction	Emptiness – you always wonder about their basis and their hope
Honesty – They always view the facts with brutal honesty	Deceived – They see the facts for what they hope they can be not for what they are
Preparation – They plan and count the cost before embarking on a path	Unprepared – They pursue the path without preparing to do what it takes to complete the journey
Integrity – They hold themselves accountable for the possibility of failure but give you credit for success and your effort	Excuses – They blame failures on the economy, unforeseen developments or bad luck on – but never on themselves
Clarity – They develop a clear plan with specific details of what must be done to win	Fuzziness – The communicate a fuzzy hope without substance for what they desire and expect to happen

We typically find one or two uncommon leaders in each of our 20 person leadership development program seminars. They share these characteristics and one that we believe is the defining feature of the determination of great leaders to achieve results. Uncommon leaders learn to define and find success from the experience of what they do and not just from the end results of what they do.

By this we mean they help people learn to find value, meaning and purpose for their work beyond just doing their work.

They drive their businesses to measure success based on the difference made and value delivered and not just by the profit it makes. Profitability is not so much necessary to meet the self-interest of the shareholders and employees who work the business but to be able to support the business in continuing to make a difference and to bring its value to its customers. This uncommon view of success is the key to what drives the high performing leaders to produce beyond what is normal.

Remember the three stone cutters. The first stone cutter was simply doing his job. He cut the stones but he didn't even envision the completed Cathedral; an honest day's work for an honest day's pay. That was his motivation. The second stone cutter was very self-focus; he wanted to be the best stone cutter in the world; you know – first to be first. The completed Cathedral didn't seem to be important to him either. The third stone cutter saw a bigger picture; he was contributing to something greater than his job. He was moved to operate with purpose and meaning beyond his task. This stone cutter saw success in being able to contribute to something great. His determination and production were likely driven by his passion to be a part of something great.

Selfless commitment and determination to a higher cause is something leaders cannot pay others to have; they cannot motivate others to have it; and they cannot direct others to have it. It is something the leader must help others find within themselves. *If dreams that wanted to be realized had minds of their own, they would find their way into the paths of uncommonly successful people.*

Author and Minister Robert H. Schuller is quoted saying *problems are not stop signs they are guide lines. Highly determined people see and act in this way; when others see the impossible, highly successful people routinely achieve the impossible.* The story of the mountain will give you a view of the impossible that denies and the determination that drives.

The Mountain

There were two warring tribes in the Andes, one that lived in the lowlands and the other high in the mountains. One day the mountain people invaded the lowlanders and as part of their plundering of the people they kidnapped a baby of one of the lowlander families and took the infant with them back up into the mountains. Now the lowlanders didn't know how to climb mountains. They didn't know any of the trails that the mountain people used and they didn't know where to find the mountain people or how to track them in the steep terrain.

Still, they sent out their best party of fighting men to climb the mountain and bring the baby home. The men tried every method they could think of to climb the mountain. They tried one trail and then another. After several days of effort they had climbed only several hundred feet. They began to feel hopeless and helpless. Eventually the lowlanders decided it was a lost cause and they prepared to return to their village below.

As they were packing their gear for the short descent, they saw the baby's mother walking toward them. They realized that she was coming down the mountain that they hadn't figured out how to climb. And then they saw that she had the baby strapped to her back. How could that be they wondered? One man greeted her and said, *we couldn't climb this mountain. How did you do this when we, the strongest and most able men in the village couldn't do it? She shrugged her should and said, It wasn't your baby.*

I'm not certain of the source of this little story but it makes a great point about strongly determined people who are driven by a great cause. They take personal ownership of all they put their hands to do; and when they do this they are typically not deterred by problems but rather guided by problems to achieve incredible results.

Determination Stage of Leadership Development

It's about! Getting Results! The leader makes winners of others by learning to produce through their efforts. When the leader demonstrates the ability to produce consistent results others have more belief in the leader for what he can do with them. The more belief they have the more commitment and potential the give. The more they give of themselves the more the leader is able to strengthen the organization and achieve more and greater results.

Leader focus: The focus of the leader during the determination stage of development is more transformational than transactional. The objective is to create more long term and longer lasting results over time.

Leader effectiveness depends on:
- Effectiveness of the leader depends on his ability to create scalable and repeatable successes;
- Ability to align others to a clearly defined vision to guide pursuit of goals and objectives;
- Ability to instill in each person a sense of purpose and meaning that spans beyond the job they must perform;
- Gaining greater commitment of others by working competently and effectively connecting with them and;

- Defining and achieving successes that not only benefit the organization but makes individuals better in the process.

People respond to the leader by:
- People connect with their hearts and respond positively because of what you have accomplished before;
- Highly motivated people are attracted to what you represent;
- People will commit more of their potential to your care and;
- People believe in your ability to continue winning.

Progression as a leader depends on:
- Your ability to scale and repeat successes;
- Creating a belief in others for the vision of what the future possibilities are for the organization and the people;
- Developing excellence and being identified for things you are the "best" at doing and;
- Maturing in the mastery of what you must BE KNOW and DO for the organization.

Just as there is an inherent and implied goodness that defines great leadership, achieving results is too a key component of leadership. You cannot disassociate results from leading. Uncommon leaders are driven by an unwavering determination and focus to achieve results. They know that the ability to achieve results first starts with winning the battle to achieve results with themselves.

Chapter Fifteen

Achieving Results

The determination and persistence of uncommon leaders distinguish them from low or average leaders. Because belief and confidence of others are important, uncommon leaders learn to produce results through the efforts of others more than by the efforts of others. They balance the social responsibilities they have toward people with the operational responsibility to get things done.

Footprints — Chapter Sixteen — Making Leaders of Others

The Footprints of Transformation

"If you ignite within man a fire deeply enough; and it burns hot enough; to create a desire compelling enough that a man would give up the desires he has for his life; to help others achieve the desires they have for their lives; you stand a good chance of developing a leader of that man". Footprints

Every day we do things that thrust us into positions or roles of leadership. Some things may be temporary such as joining a member of a sports team; other things may be permanent such as getting married, becoming a parent or accepting a new position at work. Whatever the situations are for us, we are routinely moving through life being placed in positions where we must learn to become a more effective leader.

By the time we are adults much of what we have learned, many of the habits we have developed and the impact our experiences have on us make our development as a leader a greater challenge than it should be. Our transformation into the leaders we can be is as much a process of unlearning bad habits that make us weak leaders as it is learning to become the things that will make us strong. This is why we view leadership development as a process of transformational development over time more than an act of training.

Pearls are created when a foreign body of some sort, such as a grain of sand or a parasite, finds its way into the body of an oyster. The oyster reacts to protect itself by coating the irritant with multiple layers of a substance that protects the oyster but transforms the object. The oyster's process of transforming a foreign object into a wonderful pearl can take anywhere from one to three years to complete.

Transforming people to become pearls of leaders is much like the process the oyster uses to create a pearl; a fire is lit deep within the body of a person to produce what we see as the heart of a leader. The leader's transformation process:

- Takes time! Leaders are not transformed or developed overnight;
- Takes content! There is specific content and knowledge that must be planted into the lives of future leaders to produce leaders of the future;
- Takes a process! There must be a consistent process for delivering content into the leader;
- Takes results: New knowledge, skills and abilities are created in each person to demonstrate their transformation to leaders;
- Takes measures! There are ways to measure the effectiveness of individual growth as a leader;
- Takes an environment! Transformation happens in a consistent environment where the process is nurtured to produce consistent results and;
- Takes will! Everything starts with desire. It is the key ingredient in the whole process; each person must want to

take the content, knowledge, skills and experiences and transform it into the pearl of great leadership.

I wrote Footprints after a twenty-plus year military career of personal development by great leaders for the purpose of great leadership. And with our Footprints development programs we have created and shared with you insights into the leadership environment that exists when uncommon leaders take the responsibility to develop others to become effective leaders.

The transformation stage of development is designed specifically to develop people, all people, to become leaders. It allows leaders to meet each personal and professional challenge with a transformational view – to impact what others are able to accomplish by transforming others from the inside out.

Traditional leadership development programs typically focus on teaching the leader what to do to get more from others. When we examined the footprints of uncommon leaders we found that the thing that made them uncommonly effective is their focus on getting away from leading followers by helping others to become leaders. It is an uncommon leadership paradigm focused on enabling leaders to get more from themselves as a condition of getting more from the leaders around them.

We created Footprints to be used as a personal or business leadership coach, mentor and development program. This approach ultimately serves to train skills but to grow leaders. It includes:

- Principles of Leadership: every leader must start with a foundation built on principles of effective leadership;
- The Leadership Oath: leaders must first learn never be deceived by yourself;
- The Learning Model: Learning is difficult; unlearning is even more of a challenge. Effective transformation to become an uncommon leader should follow a model of learning and development. Footprint uses the model captured in this quote by Ben Franklin – "Tell me and I forget; show me and I remember; involve me and I learn";
- The First Person Led: We help you learn to lead more effectively the *First Person*;
- The Growth Model: We establish and follow a leadership effectiveness model that simplifies your development and growth as an effectiveness leader;
- Integration: We help you blend the dynamics of leadership characteristics, traits and skills with people and business into more effective personal and professional leadership;
- Challenges to Effective Leadership: Footprints helps to identify and to overcome challenges that hinder developing uncommon leadership.

But the process of distilling effective leadership into its smaller component skills and competencies is insufficient to make you a leader. Footprints does not attempt to break effective leadership down into smaller components of traits and characteristics and so forth. These things are important elements of leadership but they are insufficient to transform you to become an effective leader.

Your transformation as a leader happens when you take a component of leading, when you take challenges on the job, when you take adversity and when you take events that happen around you and allow those things to make something new and better of you. Let me illustrate what I mean:

Chapter Sixteen — Making Leaders of Others

The Potato, Egg and the Coffee Bean

Once a daughter complained to her father that her life was miserable and that she didn't know how she was going to make it. She was tired of fighting and struggling all the time. It seemed just as one problem was solved another one soon followed. Her father, a chef, took her to the kitchen. He filled three pots with water and placed each on a high fire.

Once the three pots began to boil, he placed potatoes in one pot, eggs in the second pot and ground coffee beans in the third pot. He then let them sit and boil without saying a word to his daughter.

The daughter moaned and impatiently waited wondering what he was doing. After twenty minutes he turned off the burners. He took the potatoes out of the pot and placed them in a bowl. He pulled the eggs out and placed them a bowl. He then ladled the coffee out and placed it in a cup.

Turning to her he asked. *Daughter, what do you see? Potatoes, eggs and coffee, she hastily replied. Look closer, he said, and touch the potatoes. She did and noted that they were soft. He then asked her to take an egg and break it. After pulling off the shell, she observed the hard-boiled egg. Finally, he asked her to sip the coffee. Its rich aroma brought a smile to her face. Father, what does this mean she asked?*

He then explained that the potatoes, the eggs and coffee beans had each faced the same adversity – the boiling water. However, each one reacted differently. The potato went in strong, hard and unrelenting but in boiling water it became soft and weak.

Chapter Sixteen — Making Leaders of Others

The egg was fragile with the thin outer shell protecting its liquid interior until it was put in the boiling water. Then the inside of the egg became hard. However the ground coffee beans were unique. After they were exposed to the boiling water, they changed the water and created something new. *Which are you,* he asked his daughter?

When adversity knocks on your door how do you respond? Are you a potato, an egg or a coffee bean? In life things happen around us, things happen to us but the only thing that truly matters is what happens within us. Which one are you?

People don't make themselves leaders; a position doesn't make a person a leader; others cannot make you a leader. People become leaders when the boiling water of life connects with something in the person to create something new and different.

With Footprints we believe the best way to enable you to help transform others is to bring the boiling water to those areas of their lives that need transformation. Footprints will enable you to increase your personal effectiveness, multiply the effectiveness of others and transform the effectiveness of the business in which you lead.

The *Footprints* Process Model

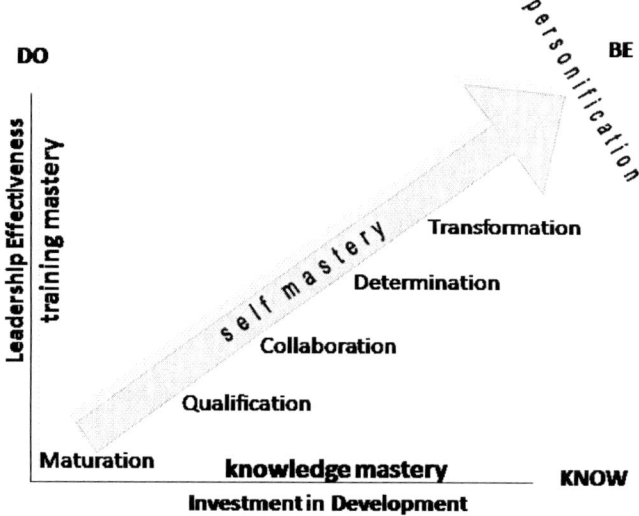

Chapter Sixteen — Making Leaders of Others

At the transformation stage of effectiveness the leader is fully operating from the transformational view of leadership. People connect with the leader at this point because of what is done for them.

It's about! Perpetuation! The focus becomes how well the leader develops others within the organization to carry on the purpose of the organization and what it means.

Leader Effectiveness depends on:
- Transformational! Developing others to be leaders not followers;
- The leader's ability to develop others for success;
- The ability to balance the leader's operational and social responsibilities with effectiveness;
- Creating and implementing change and the new roads needed for future success.

People respond to the leader by:
- People see the leader apart from the role;
- People see themselves as leaders of the leader rather than subordinates of the leader;
- People commit to the leader because of what the leader does for people and for the organization;
- People connect with their hearts instead of with their minds.

Chapter Sixteen — Making Leaders of Others

Progression as a leader depends on:

- Building a winning organization with people;
- Building a larger than life compelling vision of future possibilities;
- Reproducing in others the leadership qualities of the most effective leaders;
- Maturing in the mastery of how you develop what others must BE; what others must KNOW; and what others must DO for the organization.

Conclusion

"The question now is not whether you would follow yourself; rather it is why you believe you are ready to lead those who have no choice about who their leader is".
Footprints

There is an ancient story of how to catch a monkey. Apparently it is quite simple to do. You just put some peanuts in a jar with an opening just large enough to allow the open hand through. Place the jar anyplace where there are monkeys. The monkey will reach into the jar and grab some peanuts but he will not be able to pull his clenched fist out because the neck of the jar is too narrow. If the monkey were to just let go of the peanuts he could easily pull his hand from the jar. But he will not do that. He is too attached to the ways he has always done things. While he is preoccupied with trying to accomplish what he has always been able to accomplish he loses perspective about what is going on around him. That's when it's easy to just walk up and catch them.

We have reached a point with Footprints where you must make a choice to let go of some current or old perceptions about leading and about yourself. You cannot become an uncommon leader by simply learning new skills and competencies while still hanging on to your old ways. Transforming yourself into a leader of uncommon effectiveness requires you to change much about who you have come to be and to change the paths you've used till now to achieve the successes you enjoy today.

Common leaders will always be among us but you do not have to be one of them. They will continue trying to achieve greater success like getting peanuts from a jar with a clenched fist. And they will want to be known for being the first to do it. Common leaders are not trapped by the jar – all they need to do is let go of the peanuts and they will be free to pull back their hand. Instead they are trapped by their perspectives, by their desires, by the experiences they have learned and try to repeat. They fail to recognize that circumstances are different. The jar is smaller and their hands are bigger. They are trapped by their unwillingness to let go of a meaningless desire in order to grab hold of something of greater value; no one will say to them *hey, it's just peanuts, they won't last long anyway!*

Before reading Footprints most people think of leadership in common ways; they understand leadership in common terms; and they speak about leadership in a common language. But it is now time for you to put away the common things about leadership you have held close to you. Uncommon leadership achieves greater and more lasting results and it makes people better in the process; it never puts self-interest before the interest of others and the businesses it serves; it is great for the businesses and institutions to which it belongs and even greater for the customers of those businesses and institutions; uncommon leadership will never fail to be mature beyond what is common; to be competent beyond what is common; to relate beyond what is common; to produce beyond what is common; and to resonate beyond what is common.

Stuart Chase is quoted saying f*or those who believe, no proof is necessary. For those who don't believe, no proof is possible.* Unfortunately there is no book, no training, no seminar or no footprint of any successful leader that is proof enough of a more successful way to get common leaders to change their ways. Unless they commit to transform who they are, they are destined to repeat what they have become. You and I will stand to benefit from them or to suffer with them.

Uncommon leaders believe there is an uncommon more effective way to achieve greater results than the way common leaders so often do things today; they don't need proof of this because when they look at themselves and when they look at leaders around them they see the proof. They are hardly ever trapped by the things they do to themselves. They hardly ever create their own jars. They typically encounter and overcome the predicaments of someone else's making. The uncommon leader is able to be free of emotional attachments that become traps. They have an almost outside perspective about themselves, so that they see uncommon solutions to common situations. They look at the jar, remove the lid and pour out the contents. They are people in their environments but not of their environments, so they never lose sight of what is going on around them.

Remember, the way to change the destination of a train when it has already left the station is to change the course of the tracks.

To become a leader of uncommon effectiveness you must change the course you are taking and the course of those around you. You do this by strengthening the foundation on which you operate; by developing an uncommon sense of values, by assessing the value of the things you value and the principles by which you operate; by creating a healthier perspective about what leadership is to you; by developing purpose and vision that will drive your life and curb desires that pull you in all directions; by learning to plan more effectively – goals not born through plans are a slow path to your failure; by determining to get results through the efforts of others not by directing others; and finally by deciding to care about people. Make a difference to them and they will become the difference for you; you are developing them to be leaders not followers.

Watson transformed himself to become an uncommon leader – being the first to be first will in the end be the end for you. A full the jar of peanuts is still just peanuts. You are now at a time in your life where you must choose to put away common things that may have appeared to be gains to you and choose the excellence found in becoming a leader of uncommon effectiveness and the benefit of making uncommon leaders of the people; families, friends, and businesses around you.

And remember, in life things happen around us, things happen to us but the only thing that truly matters is what happens within us. There is no person who can make you a leader; there is no position that will make you a leader. All we can do is to put you in positions to allow you to use your life to lead. What makes you are leader is what happens within you when you decide to live your life to an uncommon standard higher than anything common to men; and when you decide your greatest cause and purpose is to give your life to the cause of others and the purposes of the business you lead; and finally, when you decide to be a right example of the greatness that can be made within all men who learn that self-interest is never the best interest.

There are some simple truths about Footprints. If you want to know where they lead - you have to follow them; and if you want to know who left them - you have to follow them. And if you follow them you are likely going to experience the things the person who left them experienced.

When all said and done what will your footprints say about you? Will the people around you look back and say *he was good for me?* Will the businesses you lead last beyond the last goal achieved and will they look back and say *he made a difference to us?* Now is when all is said and now is when all is done. It is not just your time it is your turn to rise to the level of uncommon greatness.

Good luck to you!

The Power of – PDP®

The acronym PDP® stands for Professional DynaMetric Programs. In the last chapter the importance of leadership style was stressed. Particularly important is learning more about your personal style and the strengths associated with that style. In the last chapter it was the also recommended that you utilize a powerful and accurate behavioral style assessment – **PDP ProScan®** to provide further insight to your leadership strengths. The PDP report will also help you understand other styles that are different from your own.

Before you take the survey, we want to provide more information about the history, research, and development of PDP®.

HISTORY & RESEARCH

Research on PDP® began in 1977 when Bruce Hubby, a businessman, with a strong interest in human behavior teamed with Drs. Samuel Houston and Dudley Soloman to develop the ProScan survey instrument. Their goal was to design a statistically validated, quantitative instrument that produced highly accurate results. Research involved a factor analysis process applied to descriptive adjectives used by behavioral psychologists. This study resulted in a list of 60 self-descriptive adjectives. A survey was constructed using these 60 words with responses made on a 5-point Likert scale. Based on case studies the accuracy rate has been measured at 96%.

DEVELOPMENT

PDP® was first utilized commercially in late 1978. Research and development have continued on an ongoing basis and a complete management system has been designed to utilize the highly accurate survey results. Two additional components have been developed – JobScan® and TeamScan®. These components use the ProScan® survey data to analyze and create job models and to provide team development analysis. Also a wide range of training programs for individuals and managers has been developed to enable organizations to improve their people results.

We want to give you the opportunity to benefit from taking the PDP ProScan® survey and learning more about your individual leadership style. The instructions are:

Footprints   Chapter Eighteen   Know Thyself

1. Go to the website – www.thehumanadvantage.com
2. Click on the "Take the Survey" button
3. Follow the directions as stated
4. There is a small administration fee of $35 which will require a credit card
5. You will receive a detailed "Personal Development Report

EVERYONE CAN LEAD

PDP's leadership model is based on data gathered from more than 30 years of research and validation studies. Bruce Hubby, the founder of PDP® says: "Each person has a unique leadership style that is based on a combination of traits and personal qualities. The **question is not whether a person can lead but how, or in what circumstances, will the individual be a leader**".

The four cornerstone traits measured by ProScan® are Dominance, Extroversion, Pace (patience), and Conformity (structure). The chart below provides a summary of the characteristics of each trait.

FOUR CORNERSTONE BEHAVIORAL TRAITS

| HIGH DOMINANCE | HIGH EXTROVERSION | HIGH PACE/PATIENCE | HIGH CONFORMITY |

"Control/Take charge trait"; <u>act on</u> their environment; **control oriented through THINGS**	"**Social /relational trait**"; <u>act on</u> their environment; **control oriented through PEOPLE**	"**Rate of motion/ adaptable trait**"; <u>influenced by</u> their environment; thinker; cautiously paced	"**Systems/quality assurance trait**"; <u>influenced by</u> their environment; rulebook oriented
To the point Innovators Big picture oriented Troubleshooters Outwardly secure Dislike indecisiveness Forceful decision makers	Outgoing Friendly Persuasive Empathetic Enthusiastic Talkative Motivating Optimistic Effective communicators	Persistent Cooperative Harmonious Dependable Relaxed Patient Amiable Steady Consistent Good listener	Procedural Precise Loyal Careful Conscientious Meticulous Diligent Concerned Perfectionistic

Footprints   Chapter Eighteen   Know Thyself

LOW DOMINANCE	LOW EXTROVERSION	LOW PACE (URGENCY)	*LOW CONFORMITY*
Moderate Supportive Modest Mild Gentle Understanding Humble Non-controlling Complacent	Sincere Thoughtful Contemplative Reserved Quiet Imaginative Private Confidential Unexpressive	Adaptable Likes change Fast paced Restless Impatient Hasty Sporadic Pusher Abrupt Volatile	Open minded Curious Generalist Non-detailed Free spirited Flexible Uninhibited Non-conforming Anti-bureaucratic

©1984, Revised July 1998 PDP, Inc. Woodland Park, Colorado USA

The chart below shows how each of the four cornerstone traits measured by PDP® has unique leadership strengths and areas to develop:

Footprints   Chapter Eighteen   Know Thyself

Developing Effective Leadership Actions

When the leader has a high trait of **DOMINANCE**		When the leader has a high trait of **EXTROVERSION**	
Key Strengths	Decisive Direct Objective Innovative Takes charge Delegates responsibility Organizes	Key Strengths	Inspire Motivate Coach Delegate authority and responsibility Sell/Persuade Optimistic
Natural Responses	Authoritative Controlling	Natural Responses	People pleaser Defer decision Too trusting
Extreme Responses	Dictatorial Steamroll	Extreme Responses	Verbal attack Overpower with persuasion
Learned Responses to match situation	Delegate authority Listen to ideas of others Participate in teamwork	Learned Responses to match situation	More direct and confrontational Objectivity Authoritative
When the leader has a high trait of **PACE**		When the leader has a high trait of **CONFORMITY**	
Key Strengths	Listen Instruct and Teach Collaborate Persistence Mediate	Key Strengths	Maintain systems Hold to standards Process oriented Accuracy of details
Natural Responses	Keep status-quo Methodical approach Wait for agreement	Natural Responses	Refer to rule book and policy manual Require a chain of command Double check work and decisions
Extreme Responses	Avoid conflict Get even later Resist change	Extreme Responses	Bury critics with facts Inflexible Bottle-neck work flow
Learned Responses to match situation	Take charge Assertive Accept and make rapid changes	Learned Responses to match situation	Take justified risks Adapt to unproven methods

© 1984, Revised 2010, PDP, Inc., Colorado Springs, Colorado USA

| Footprints | Chapter Eighteen | Know Thyself |

These two charts provide a brief look at the four basic traits that influence our behavior. The PDP ProScan® Personal development report will provide a more in depth look at these dimensions. An effective leader understands and appreciates their strengths but also realizes that their natural style does not fit every situation. Being an effective leader requires a high level of self-awareness and authenticity. It takes dedication to personal growth. Take time now to discover more about yourself'

You can find out which of these traits is your primary strength by taking the ProScan survey.

Chapter Nineteen

About The Transforming Leader

Footprints was written and our Transforming Leader Development Programs designed to be a tool leaders use to develop others to become leaders. Our services include:

- Corporate Leadership Development Seminars and Executive Intensives;
- Annual Leadership Development Seminars for individuals and small groups from different organizations;
- Corporate and team business planning seminars;
- Inspirational leadership development and planning guest speaking event support and;
- Uniquely designed corporate programs focused on improving leadership effectiveness and developing business competence to execute more effectively.

To learn more about the Footprints Programs, please email, write or call us at:

The Transforming Leader

Footprints of the Uncommon Leader

1825 West Walnut Hill Lane

Suite 120

Irving, Texas 75038

Email: TTL@transformingleader.com.

972.331.2631

Chapter Nineteen

About the Author

Allen Forte has been a leading developer of People and Business Strategy for more than twenty years. He has built a strong reputation for designing and implementing strategic leadership development and business management processes needed to sustain a high level of individual and business success.

The seeds and inspiration for writing Footprints were planted and manifested during a very successful twenty-plus year military career where Allen was noted for designing and developing high level people and business processes and strategies. It was through The Transforming Leader that Footprints was formally launched in the business sector in 2003. Footprints is a unique approach to helping ordinary people learn to become uncommon leaders.

In March 2000, Allen retired from a very successful career as an officer in our nation's military where he rose to the level of senior people and business strategist with the Army Pentagon. His own personal and professional development and nurturing makes him uniquely suited to take an uncommonly effective approach to developing people and businesses to become uncommon developers of leaders, in business planning and execution and in developing strong lasting organizations.

Allen holds a Master's Degree from The George Washington University, Washington, DC, an undergraduate from Columbus State University, Columbus Georgia. He is also a graduate of the Army Center for Human Resources Professionals, The Army Command and General Staff College and The National Defense University with a concentration in Long Range Strategic Planning. During his time with the Defense Department, Allen was a noted leader in developing leaders, strategic thinking and in the formulation of business strategy.